EXCAVATION OF THE EARLY VILLAGE FARMING COMMUNITIES OF PANDURAJAR DHIBI WEST BENGAL

A Case Study

EXCAVATION OF THE EARLY VILLAGE FARMING COMMUNITIES OF PANDURAJAR DHIBI WEST BENGAL

A Case Study

Tapas Bandyopadhyay

PATHAK PUBLISHER AND DISTRIBUTORS
New Delhi (INDIA)

Excavation of The Early Village Farming Communities of Pandurajar Dhibi West Bengal: A Case Study

Author : Tapas Bandyopadhyay

ISBN : 978-93-91952-34-1

Price : 1500/-

First Edition: 2023

Published by :
PATHAK PUBLISHER AND DISTRIBUTORS
E-6/33c & 34, Ground Floor, Sangam Vihar
New Delhi-110080
E-mail: pathakppd@gmail.com

Typographic Design by: G. R. Sharma

CONTENTS

PREFACE

The main objective of the present work is to write a simple report on the material remains of Early Village Farming (E.V.F.) communities, tentatively emerged around second half of the second millenium B.C. in West Bengal, with special reference to excavation at Pandurajar Dhibi, Burdwan, West Bengal. The compilation of reported materials other than Pandurajar Dhibi, presented in this work is an attempt coming from my personal initiative to the subject since my joining in the Directorate of Archaeology & Museums (D.A.& M.), West Bengal. The special initiative as well as working interest on the excavated materials of Pandurajar Dhibi has been taken when State Archaeological Museum (S.A.M.) at Behala, Kolkata started functioning in the year 1980. Fortunately the Directorate has chosen me for cataloguing the archaeological objects and the display works of collected antiquities of the said museum in January 1986, though my career began as a Cataloguer since December 1980, at Hazarduari Palace, Murshidabad under the same Directorate.

It was from 1986, I had an opportunity to conceive diverse materials coming from different parts of West Bengal recorded by the D.A.& M. In turn, with the data, I had enough scope to trace it's relationship with rise and growth of society in ancient Bengal through the ages. Interestingly the collected materials of Protohistoric period attract much rather than other antiquities ranging from Prehistory to Premodern period. Subsequently in the year 2000-2001, I have able to come out with a specific research frame work which ultimately took shape as Ph. D. research topic. The present work is the culmination of research material housed in the State Archaeological Museum, W.B., though the enormous data in the form of artefacts certainly has a route towards the understanding of village society particularly through the ages.

The B.R.W. cultural phase of West Bengal archaeology is also termed as Ferro - chalcolithic / Iron Age, scattered over on the different parts of the region specially covering the districts of Bankura, Birbhum, Burdwan and undivided Medinipur forms a matrix which is essentially a formative stage of farming and village cultural society.

The distribution of BRW sites in West Bengal helps us to know the emergence of early farming settlements and the way of sedantism in contemporary life. If we have a look on the comparison of such sites, we may correctly assume the pattern of concentration of settlement including the nucleus and the periferial one. The phase received much attention by the scholar for the reconstruction of BRW society and its relationship with the conventional frame work i.e., Neo-chalcolithic, Chalcolithic and Iron. Similarly the material remains of this period as well as my personal experience with the antiquities of Pandurajar Dhibi, also attract me to work with some new ideas and opinion. Though we have limitations to interpret excavated and explored data, it is also certain that we have may difficulty to follow the earlier chrono-cultural frame work and it's association with BRW material remains. Therefore my research interest has always been searching a set of terminology to put my data for the convenience of the scholarly world. Finally I came out with the term for the present topic i.e. "The Early Village Farming Communities of West Bengal : A Case Study (The Survey of Archaeological Remains at Pandurajar Dhibi, Burdwan District)".

The main issue of this present work are encapsulated in the title of chapter and sub chapter of this work. Emergence of Neolithic Society in West Bengal is truly the focus of this volume, whether by the end of this so called Neolithic society as well as Proto historic community or early village farmers have really emerged in West Bengal. The present work also tried to discribe behavioural pattern of Late Mesolithic society (The Mesolithic survivals) and transition between our conventionally defined notions of the Mesolithic - Neolithic and so called Chalcolithic or Protohistoric periods. Principally, the society based on ceramic using hunter-gatherer and farming communities that relied on the mixture of both with limited farming.

Even though the movement of agricultural activities across the Middle ganga valley was a coincedence and have no relation to the components available in the finding of the chhotonagpur hunter-gatherers. They were soon to fill it's impact, which must have begun by chance-encounter between foreagers of Bankura, Purulia and adjoining Burdwan farmers of Middle and Lower ganga valley. In this context it is to be noted that the Pandurajar Dhibi played an important role to develop the village society with mixed economy.

Finally, it developed into exchange of commodities into trade and the passage of ideas, information and probabely genes between the communities of farmers in and around the Ajay, Damodar and the Dwarakeswar valley. The hunter-gatherer of lateritic Bengal, who were the users of Microliths probabely confronted with conflict and violence. It is unique to visualise with our findings specially recorded from Pandurajar Dhibi and Pakhanna, the hunter-gatherers were transformed by these contacts and gradually merged with the large scale development of the ganga valley.

LIST OF ILLUSTRATION

LIST OF ABBREVIATION

1. Early village Farming — EVF.
2. Directorate of Archaeology & Museums — D.A. & M.
3. State Archaeological Museum — S.A.M.
4. Black and Red ware — BRW.
5. Black ware — BW.
6. Red ware — RW.
7. Baneswar Danga — BND.
8. Bharatpur — BTP.
9. Bhhiri — BHR.
10. Charul — CRL.
11. Hat-tikra — HTK.
12. Dihar — DHR.
13. Mahisdal — MSD.
14. Mogalmari — MGM
15. Mangalkot — MGK.
16. Nanur — NNR.
17. Salkhana/Haraipur — SLN / HPR.
18. Tulshipur — TLP
19. Tamluk — TLK.
20. Pakhanna — PKN.
21. Pandurajar — Dhibi

22. Indian Archaeology - A Review — IAR.
23. Archaeological Survey of India — ASI
24. West Bengal District Gazetters — WBDG.
25. Zoological Survey of India — ZSI.
26. Botanical Sruvey of India — BSI.

ACKNOWLEDGEMENTS

I recall with gratitude the name of late Paresh Chandra Dasgupta, former director of my Directorate who have played a significant role in the genesis of this work. I am indebted to those who have shared a rigour of my fieldwork especially late Pratip Mitra, former keeper State Archaeological Museum, late Sudhin De, exploration assistant, Dilip Roy Catelouger and late Bishwanath Samanta. Thanks are due to late Nepal Chandra Bhattacharjee and late Anil Karmakar, Mr. Pratul Sen, surveyor and Ranjit Sen, Artist photographer, and also thankful to Debimadhob Chakraborty, Kaushik Halder and Prakash Maity for their academic support. In recent years I received a lot of inspiration from late Prof. Amita Ray, late Prof. Anil Chnadra Pal, late Dr. Asok Dutta and Prof. Rupendra kumar Chattopadhyay of department of Archaeology, University of Calcutta.

Prof. Rupendra Kumar Chattopadhyay, my mentor and guide of this whole work and whatever I have achieved is due to his strong academic support, he has always inspired me and has constantly responded from Calcutta university and Presidency University, Kolkata.

I am also indebted to Emeritus Prof. Dilip Kumar Chakrabarti and late D.K. Bhattacharya for their constant inspiration and mental support for this auspicious publication.

I acknowledge my indebtedness to my wife smt. Shampa Banerjee, daughter Tapahsama and my student Abhishek Roy, who have played marvellous role in my struggling academic career. Heartfelt thanks to them for their constant love and silence support and they are the source of stability in my life. I am also thankful to Dr. Kumkum Banerjee for pottery documentation and Japashree Kar Chowdhury for bone tool drawing.

Finally, I acknowledge the valuable services rendered by Mr. Swapan Mukherjee, State Archives Govt. of West Bengal and Mr. Bholanath Mukherjee, Caps Micrographics, Kolkata, for their splendid help and assistance. I am also in a position to offer my tribute to Pathak Publisher and Distributors, New Delhi, India, of this noble work.

1

INTRODUCTION

The diversity of Indian physiography over various regions harboured different types of culture. In turn, each distinct character of culture played a vital role in the changing pattern of economy & society. The importance of religious order in different regional agrarian base, might have played an important role towards the cultural unity of Indian life as a whole. The exploitation of natural resources through the manoeuvering of man power resulted the entire regional space to achieve the inter-regional exchange net work through the process of behavioural pattern, subsistance economy and religious belief and practice. However, the environmental feature and ecological factors are the major contents, responsible for the emergence of culture and the formulation of incipient stage of society which is known as formative stage of our village society. The changing pattern of exploitation of natural resources in the innovation of new technology, excellerated the growth of settlement and economic base depending on the knowledge of articulation in different geographical areas.

In this context, it is worth mentioning that K.M.Panikkar has observed, "History may well conceived as the pressure of the nomad - both of the land and sea - against civilization. Those countries which stand directly in the way of these nomads are destroyed and broken from time to time. Those that are protected by geography, received a back wash and after a turmoil, settled down again".[1]

We have a very limited data to visualise the palaeo- environmental feature of our study area and its relationship with the exploitation of environmental resources. The archaeological discoveries are always helping us to improve our knowledge about the relationship between man & environment in the past. The present day topography and the entire eco-system in and around Ajay- Damodar valley, where our study area located, certainly had a root in the exploitation history of this regional environment.

The broad spectrum analysis of the entire physiography and report base for the survival of ancient population in this area suggest, that the following set up of environmental feature certainly played an important role for the growth of the changing pattern of demography & early settlements.

1) The landscape along the peripheral region where we can locate a forest cover along with ores for metal and minerals.
2) The undulating lateritic track, where one could easily trace the metal bearing ore for the procurement of metal by the ancient people including the early dwellers of Pandurajar Dhibi.
3) The alluvial flood plains and the arable landscape of fertile soil formation along the river Ajay and Damodar is essentially a formation gifted to the first settlers of Pandurajar Dhibi for the beginning of farming and agriculture.
4) The major and minor rivers including their tributory in and around Mangalkot also played an important role for the procurement of water resources including acquatic, plant and animals.

The embayments of the Indo-Gangetic wide alluvium extended further south against the central Indian plateau, characterized by ridges of hills, steep embankments of rivers and forests. Such physical features are also presented by the chhotonagpur plateau of Jharkhand and it's territorial extension in Bihar and West Bengal. The physical isolation of these regions have helped the inhabitants in maintaining their primitive character and way of life for a long time. Subba Rao has, therefore, labelled the regions as areas of isolation.[2] Although in the recent years, the Subba Rao concept may not be accepted in some cases rather than it's broad generalisation. In sharp opposition to above areas, we find an altogether different picture in the important river basins which render a considerable fertile area and there by attract people to colonise it. The indo-gangetic plain along with it's extension towards east, left the rich fertile land with a very favourable rainfall, enable the people to have a surplus output by exploiting the agricultural potentiality. Surplus economy is a primary requisite for speedy development of any culture or civilization. These areas have, therefore, being called as "Areas of attraction". Thus the whole pattern of development of material culture in India may be defined as one of the horizontal expansion of the higher cultures, leading to a displacement, contraction and isolation of the lower culture, in different parts of the country, at different cultural level.[3]

The extensive explorations and intensive excavations under taken through out the length and breadth of India have succeeded in unearthing a plethora of new evidences as well as created certain new problems too. The cultural significance of Black and Red ware is such a problem, yet to be solved properly.

The Black and Red ware first designated as such by Sir. Mortimer Wheeler.[4] It was supposed to belong to Early Historical Horizon, and termed as the Satavahana Ware for a long time. However, the problem has received a new dimension because of recent excavation, especially in Gujrat, Rajasthan, Madhya Pradesh, Bihar, West Bengal, Maharashtra and Karnataka. The excavation in those areas have confirmed the discovery of this ware in the protohistoric context.

Early work on protohistoric India was essentially carried out by Deccan College under the Leadership of Professor H. D. Sankalia. The excavation at Ahar in Rajasthan established the protohistoric sequence of this region based on major and minor excavated materials from Aharian sites.[5]

Scholars carried out extensive excavation and exploration in different parts of Gujrat for establising protohistoric sequence. Both Rajasthan and Gujrat had association with Black and Red ware in the context of early village farming community. [6]

The later stage of development and its relationship with early village farming community could be understoood with the discovery of some material remains from other parts of India i.e. Karnataka regions[7] (Brahmagiri, Maski, Hallur, Piklihal, Tekkalakota), Panjab[8] (Bara, Rupar, Bhagawanpur) & Hariyana upper[9] (Attaranjikhera), Middle[10] (Noh), and Lower ganga valley[11] (Pandurajar Dhibi, Baneswardanga) sites. In addition Malwa region also received some importance.

The perspective of Indian Archaeology gradually changed its mode of working and therefore again the Deccan College, Pune, took the initiative to execute more excavation of Early Village Farming sites in Malwa region, Deccan Plateau and Aravalli. It is worth mentioning that S.B.Deo, S.A.Shali and M.K.Dhawalikar took special attention to draw a long term programme related to the sequence of a region and spread of culture from one region to other. Therefore the sites like Kayatha, Navdatoli of the Malwa region, Sawalda, Daimabad, Jorwe and Inamgaon in the Deccan plateau, Balathal in Rajasthan were excavated for rendering a long sequence of early village farming since Kayatha culture (Kayatha - Sawalda - Malwa - Jorwe - Diamabad).

In the recent years, scholars like Dhawalikar and Sindhe studied the region in terms of settlement Archaeology and put data for the better understanding of the society as a whole since the emergence of ceramic based culture. In the same area, the work of

B. K. Thapar on Prakash and Jorwe deserve special mention. Similarly, the cultural contour of the other parts of the country, representing early village farming activity could be realised with the evidence of Bara in Panjab, Siswal & Mitathal in Haryana, Late - Haraappan BRW - OCP Narhan in upper and middle ganga valley and finally the BRW culture of Bengal, Bihar and Orissa extended our scope of research on the same topic. Moreover, the entire cultural Milieu related to the beginning of early village settlement, and maturity towards intensification of Pastoralism and Agriculture, added our knowledge about the growth of Indian village society.

Black and Red ware, excepting O.C.P. has been found in association with practically all principal ceramic tradition of ancient India. These varied association have thus blessed this ware with a versetile contextual personality which can amply be gleaned from the fact that it has been reported right from the early level of Harappan period, down to late levels of early historical periods of ancient India.[13] The principal sites which have yielded Black and Red ware in Neolithic contexts are Piklihal, Raichur District : Karnataka, Koldihwa, Allahabad District : U.P. and Chirand, Saran District : Bihar. In the context of early village farming community, this ware has been found in the earliest levels of Lothal, Navdatoli, Chandoli, Inamgaon, Songaon, Bahal, and Diamabad in Maharashtra. The middle ganga valley played an important role for the extension of village farming culture to East. Therefore, the rise and development of this epoch should be visualised with the finding recorded from the Lower ganga valley, may closely connected with the development of its counterpart towards west.

Post independence research work on BRW has proved the existence of early village farming community in the Districts of Murshidabad, Birbhum, Bankura, Bardhaman and undivided Medinipur[14]. The choice of people during the contemporary period mainly concentrated in the old alluvial area while they are less interested in the areas of new alluvial laterite belt. Thus we may assume that the first agricultural folk of West Bengal settled over old alluvial, (Vindhyan alluvium) brought down by rivers originating in the chhotonagpur plateau.

The BRW phase in West Bengal marks the first well documented village settlement among the other States of India. An earlier phase of such settlement has been reported only from Pandurajar Dhibi. There is no earlier level, has yet been identified like Bihar and Orissa[15]. Partition of India has taken away a large portion of Bengal from us, and while speaking about Bengal Archaeology, we have to concentrate our attention in present West Bengal.

Since the emergence of the Directorate of Archaeology and Museums, West Bengal in 1960, vigorous activities have been noticed in the field of exploration, excavation and conservation as well as display. Other institutions responsible for such endeavour include the works of Eastern Circle of Archaeological Survey of India, Department of Ancient Indian History & Culture, Department of Archaeology, Calcutta University, Department of Anthropology, Calcutta University. They have supervised also the discovery and subsequent excavation of a good number of proto historic Black and Red ware sites on the banks of Punarbhaba, Ganga, Bhagirathi, Mayurakshi, Kopai, Ajay, Kunoor, Dwarakeswar, Damodar, Silai and Kansai.[15]

The copper hoard culture served the role of an inter mediary stage between Harappa & Black and Red Ware phase in India. The culture is characterised by the occurrence of Axes, Bar-celts, Shouldered celts, Antenne swords, Anthropomorphic figures etc in copper with an ochrous red ware, totally discoloured. Few copper implements has been discovered in West Bengal from Tamajhuri, Chatla, and Parihati of Medinipur district. The authors of the copper hoard culture is yet to be settled in West Bengal on a scientific basis.

While comparing the Black and Red ware sites in Eastern India, it is confirmed that the entire early village farming community in Eastern India was possibly homogenous in form. Pandurajar Dhibi was the first Black and Red ware site probed for excavation by the Directorate of Archaeology & Museums, Government of West Bengal under the supervision of Shri Paresh Chandra Dasgupta (1962-65) and later by Dr. Shyam Chand Mukherjee (1985). Regarding the scope and source material of the present work, apart from the published and unpublished reports of excavated and explored BRW- sites of West Bengal, the excavated materials from Pandurajar Dhibi will be studied to get a somehow coherent picture of the society of the early village farming communities and their association with Black and Red ware.

Late Paresh Chandra Dasgupta, the excavator of Pandurajar Dhibi made an attempt to highlight several issues observed during his working period. According to him, it reveal remote antiquity of the copper age civilization of the Ajay and Damodar valley & speak a highly developed and organised state of society whose economy, as it appears to be based on trade with lands beyond the sea besides cultivation of rice, manufacturing of pottery, rearing of cattles and pits and hunting[16]. This observation helped us to lay the foundation of research on the present topic. But it is very difficult to accept Dasgupta's hypothesis in real term and in the present attempt, we have turn our attention in different ways.

NOTES AND REFERENCES

1. K. M. Pannikkar : Geographical Factors in Indian History, Bombay- 1955, Page : 5 - 6.
2. B. Subbarao : The personality of India, Baroda, 1958, Page : 9.
3. B. Subbarao : op. cit, Page : 12.
4. D. P. Agrawal : Protohistoric chronology technology and ecological factors : A synthesis, Puratattva : No-1, 1967-68, Page : 22.

5. D. P. Agrawal : C - 14 Dates, Banas Culture and the Aryan, Current Science : 35, March - 5, 1966, Page - 114.

6. H. D. Sankalia : Excavation at Ahar (Tambavati), Poona - 1969.

7. S. R. Rao (a) : Lothal and the Indus Civilization, Bombay, 1973, Page-60.

   S. R. Rao (b) : Excavation at Rangpur and other Exploration in Gujrat, Ancient India No : 1963. Page - 207, 190, 189, 188.

8. (a) R. N. Mehta & S. N. Choudhury, Excavation at Jokha, Baroda, 1971.

   (b) H. D. Sankalia, Prehistory and Protohistory of India & Pakistan, Poona, 1974, Page - 360.

   (c) Indian Archaeology : A Review, 1955-56, 1956-57, 1958-59, 1963-64.

9. (a) Ancient India : No - 22, New Delhi.

   (b) M. Wheeler, Ancient India : No - 4, New Delhi.

   (c) B. K. Thapar, Ancient India : No - 13, New Delhi 1957.

   (d) Indian Archaeology : A review,1956-57, Page : 30.

   (e) B. B. Lal, Ancient India : No - 5, New Delhi, 1949.

   (f) B. K. Thapar, Ancient India : No - 8, Page : 3 - 16.

   (g) M. S. Nagaraja Rao : Protohistoric cultures of the Tungabhadra Valley-A report on Hallur Excavations, 1971.

10. Indian Archaeology : A review. 1953-54. Page : 7. 1658-59. Page : 52. 1962-63 Page : 43. 1963-64. Page : 45.

11. Indian Archaeology : A review. 1962-63. Page : 43.

    1963-64, Page : 45.

12. Indian Archaeology : A review 1972-73.

    Page : 7, 36.

13. P. C. Dasgupta : Excavation at Pandurajar Dhibi, 1964, Kolkata, Page - 44.

14. H. N. Singh : History and Archaeology of Black and Red Ware (Chalcolithic Period) Delhi, 1982, Page : 21 - 39.

15. D. K. Chakrabarti & others : Black and Red Ware Settlement in West Bengal. South Asian Studies, 9, 1993.

16. P. C. Dasgupta : Excavation at Pandurajar Dhibi, 1964, Kolkata, Page : 45.

2

THE DISCOVERY OF BLACK AND RED WARE SITES IN WEST BENGAL

The archaeologists and orientologists of India tabooed West Bengal as terra-incognita, particularly in respect of prehistoric and protohistoric archaeology during the days before and after independence inspite of its immence archaeological possibilities.[1] But vigorous activities have been noticed and exploration - excavation have been systematically carried out since the emergence of the Directorate of Archaeology & Museums, West Bengal in 1960. The other institutional efforts included works of the Department of Archaeology and Anthropology, University of Calcutta and Eastern Circle of Archaeological Survey of India.

The exploration has revealed that the upland of Bengal, meeting escarpment of the chhotonagpur plateau in the western fringe of West Bengal and watered Mayurakshi in the north and the suvarnarekha in the south with a medial zone represented by the Kangshavati and Damodar. It was the natural homeland of our premitive ancestors in the dawn of civilization in West Bengal.[2] The record of exploration envisages the occurrence of Black and Red ware from Rupar in the North to Adichanallur in the South and Desalpur in the West to Pandurajar Dhibi in the East, with a time bracket ranging from the middle of 3rd, m.m. B.C. down to the beginning of the Christian era.[3] The Black and Red Ware using people of West Bengal are dated to post Harappan period which has marked the first well documented chapter of village settlements in the state.[4] Index study of Black and Red Ware settlements in West Bengal in 1993 under the joint collaboration of Directorate of Archaeology & Museums, W. B., Cambridge University of United Kingdom and Delhi University had spotted the Districts of Bardhaman, Bankura, Birbhum, Purva-medinipur, Pashchim-medinipur and Murshidabad as the habitat of early village farming communities in West Bengal.[5]

Among the explored sites, 15 only were subjected to excavation by different Government and Autonomous authority. The name of the excavated sites are as follows.,

	Name of the Site	Year of excavation	Name of Institution
1.	Baneswar Danga,Bardhaman	1974	Directorate of Archaeology & Museums, Government of West Bengal.
2.	Bharatpur, Bardhaman	1974-75	Archaeological Survey of India, Eastern Circle & University of Bardhaman, W. B.
3.	Bahiri, Birbhum	1981-82	Department of History, Delhi University
4.	Charul, Bardhaman	2003	Directorate of Archaeology & Museums. Govt. of West Bengal
5.	Hat-tikra (Hatikira), Birbhum	1987-88	Department of A.I.H.C. & Archaeology, Visva Bharati, Santiniketan, Bolpur, Birbhum.
6.	Dihar, Bankura	1983-85	Department of Archaeology, University of Calcutta
7.	Mahisdal, Birbhum	1964-65	Archaeological Survey of India, Eastern Circle
8.	Mogalmari, Danton, Purva-	2003-04	Department of Archaeology, Medinipur. University of Calcutta
9.	Mangalkot, Bardhaman	1986-89	Department of Archaeology, University of Calcutta
10.	Nanur, Birbhum	1945	Ashutosh Museum, University of Calcutta, and explored later by the D.A. & M, West Bengal to prove the existence of Black and Red Ware.
11.	Salkhana / Haraipur, Birbhum. (Yakher-Danga)	1967-68	Archaeological Survey of India, Easter Circle.

12.	Tulshipur, Bankura.	1968	Archaeological Survey of India, Eastern Circle & Melbourne University, Australia.
13.	Tamluk, Purva Medinipur	1940,1955 & 1973 - 74	Archaeological Survey of India, Eastern Circle.
14.	Pakhanna, Bankura	2002-03	Department of Archaeology, University of Calcutta.
15.	Pandurajar Dhibi, Burdhamana	1962-65 & 1985	Directorate of Archaeology and Museums, Govt of West Bengal

Brief Summery on Excavations

1. Bharatpur: A small scale excavation was conducted at Bharatpur, District Bardhaman, Jointly by the Eastern Circle of the Archaeological Survey of India and the University of Burdwan. The site lies on the left bank of the Damodar, about 7 - kms south - east of Panagarh railway station. Three seasons of excavation (1971-72, 1972-73, 1973-74) has yielded a four fold sequence from early village farming deposition to the remnants of a stupa in early - historic times.

The second season of excavation (1972-73) has yielded the evidence of proto-historic deposition in a trench measuring 10 x 10 mts on the western and southern peripheri of the mound. The material remains envisages apart from Buddhist Stupa, the evidence of neo-chalcolithic habitation at the bottom followed by an early iron age culture after which the site was deserted till the construction of a stupa. The elements of early village farming community has been realised from the material evidence like plain and painted Black and Red ware, Black on Red ware and Buff on Red wares. The shapes represented here bears adequate similarities with the pottery of Pandurajar Dhibi & Mahishdal. The linear designs of painted pottery mainly consisted of wavy line in groups, vertical and horizontal bands and oblique strokes. Among the other finds, mantion may be made of objects of bone and antlers, neolithic celts, microliths and beads of semi-precious stones. The copper objects are very few in number. No house plan of this culture was encountered since the excavation was on a limited scale. Lastly a couple of open variety "Hearth", approximately 50 cms in diameter, were noticed in two succeeding habitation layers. (6).

Baneswar Danga: The archaeological site of Baneswar Danga situated in the village of Barabelun, P. S. Bhatar, District : Bardhaman. The excavation work was began in April

1974 and continued upto August 1974 under the supervision of Late Paresh Chandra Dasgupta, Director of Archaeology and Museums, Govt. of West Bengal.

The size of the mound at the time of excavation was 84 mts. E-W X 63 mts N-S. In all, four trenches were laid out covering the steep slopes and crest of the mound --------- BND. I, to the eastern side of the Baneswar Siva temple, measuring 6 mts X 5 mts; BND II to east of the temple, measuring 6 mts X 5 mts; BND III & IV to the east of the temple and to the north of BND I, measuring 5 mts X 2.50 mts each. The mound has a slope in southern side. The aim of the digging was to unravel the culture sequences and determining the date of introduction of iron at the site. But due to limited nature of digging, a complete picture of all the phases could not be obtained.

There are in all five periods, intervened by breaks between periods I & II and in between period III & IV. The period III of the site is a transitional phase, in as much as iron was introduced at the site during that time. At the same time, the habitation of Baneswar Danga came to an end in period III with the advent of Iron using people after a massive conflagration.

The early village farmers of Baneswar Danga were acquainted with the wheel turned pottery including storage jars, vases, bowls, channel spouted bowls, dishes on stand, basins, cups, tall beaker like tumblers, trumpet or tulip shaped vases, lids, lotas & dishes. Besides perforated vessels, jars & vases having paddy husk impression on the core, occurrence of terracota figurineof elephants, objects of bone and copper and few microlithic tools indicate the existence of a village farming community at the site in period I. The bone tool include point, arrow - head, engraver etc. suggested hunting beside a pastoral economy.

Period II of Baneswardanga has yielded microliths including point, borer, engraver, polished objects, beads of semi - precious stone, copper ring, besides jars, vases, bowls, tumblers, basins, lotas, lids in plain and painted red slipped ware, BRW, Grey ware, Black slipped ware etc.

The cultural assemblage of period III consists of jars, bowls, lotas, vases, basins, cups and dishes in red slipped ware, Grey ware, Black slipped ware, objects of bone and iron, beads of semi precious stone and terracotta objects aside animal bones.

The early village farmers of Baneswardanga lived in huts having reed - screened and mud - plastered walls and floors of beaten moorum or lime plastered in period I only. In period II, lime plastered gobri floors were prepared. In period III and IV lime plastered floors noticed frequently. Some times post holes were noticed in these floors probably for raising huts or tying the rope of domesticated animals, who supplied food articles in the form of meat and other substances.

The food habit of the early dwellers of the site consist of rice, fish, turtle and meat. The evidence of rice may be observed from the paddy husk impressions on the core of the pottery. They also practiced fishing and hunting. No human burial or skeleton remains have been unearthed from the site.

The copper had a limited usein this site. No copper object has been recovered from period I. A single piece of copper ring has been recovered from period II, while period III witnessed the occurrence of 3 - copper beads of disc shape, 1 fragmentary copper bangle and ear ornament.

Among the notworthy faunal remains, mention may be made of the bones of humped cattle, ordinary cattle, buffalo, deer, pig, horse, dog, neil-gai, wolf, jungle cat, turtle, jungle fowl and fish. The flesh as well as bones of the aforesaid animals & birds provided animal protein to the contemporary village folks. Few of these animals and birds were domesticated for procuring their by product. After analysing bone samples, it has been observed that the people used split bones of animals for making tools like engravers, borers, arrowheads and points, some of which are broken due to constant use. Of the 14 - bone tools, five belonged to period I & nine to period It is absent in period III & IV.

Iron slags and objects are recovered from period III & IV. As many as five iron objects including swords, spear - head are noteworthy. They are mostly fragile and mutilated and the evidence regarding the process of iron smelting is very poor.

The inhabitants of the site used to wear ornament of semi - precious stones like agate, faience, carnelian etc. Of these types, terracotta (clay) objects seems to have been very common and semi - precious stones came next. The use of copper was very rare. Of the 25 - beads, excavated from the site, 11 were of terracotta, 12 of semi - precious stone and 2 of copper. The site is very poor in terracotta object and they offered their existence in period I & II only.

The excavation at Baneswardanga has yielded coarse red ware, coarse black and red ware, coarse black and micaceous red ware with a sandy fabric, besides few fragments of a fine red slipped ware and black and red ware from period I. Some of the coarse red and grey wares bore husk impressions on their core. Examples of perforated vases in black and red ware were slightly higher than those made in red ware. The other important types of black and red ware includes trumpet and inverted helmet shaped or tulip shaped vases, bowls on stand, tumblers and dishes. The storage jars, cooking vessel, lotas and bowls were made in coarse red, coarse grey coarse black ware. The channel spouted bowls occurred maximum in black ware and very few in BRW. Some times, the pots were painted having geometric designs while the incised motifs appeared only on black slipped ware. Period II of the site was devoid of any painted pottery. But the percentage of BRW was increased in number while the red ware remained same. The types & shapes consisted of jars, dishes, bowls, tumblers, trumpt shaped or tulip shaped flower vase, bowls on stand and channel spouted bowl, all made in black and red, black, and red ware. Our observation also suggest an increase in the number of bowls on stand and decrease in the number of tumblers, trumpet shaped vase and bowl. It has been noticed also that perforated vase occurred only in red ware. (7)

Bahiri : The archaeological site of Bahiri is situated on the East of Bolepur and North of Ajay river was excavated by Delhi University in 1981-82 under the supervision of Prof. D. K. Chakrabarti.

The protohistoric assemblage consist of BRW, RW, Buff ware, bone tools, copper ring and wires, iron implements, beads of stone and terracotta along with some painted pottery.

The C_{14} analysis of charcoal sample suggest a date of C. 960 B. C. to C. 890 B. C. which once again proved the use of iron from 1000 B.C. (8)

Charul : The Directorate of Archaeology and Museums, Government of West Bengal conducted trial diggings at Charul on the Brahmani river valley in Katwa subdivision of Bardhaman district. There is sporadic occurrence of Black and Red ware at a depth of 1.20 - 2.00 mts. (9)

Hatikhera : The site is situated 1 km west of present village Hatikhera on the right bank of river Bakreswar. It was subject to excavation by the Department of Ancient History, Culture and Archaeology, Visva Bharati University, Shantiniketan. The mound measures 190 mts from North to South and rises 2 to 2.50 mts from the surrounding ground level. It is located in the overlapping zone of the laterite upland and the alluvium zone.

The aim of the excavation was to find out whether the village farming culture played any role in the growth of later development and to ascertain the culture sequence of the site after employing multidisciplinary approaches in excavation.

There are altogether 4 - trenches laid at the four strategic points envisages a maximum deposit of 2.40 mts of habitational phase of BRW - culture followed by iron users of Period II. There is neither a hiatus nor a transitional phase intervened between the two periods.

The important potteries from period I are BRW, Grey ware, Black-slipped ware, Buff ware, envisaging bowls, vases and dish beside the usual occurrence of channel spouted bowl. The other important objects included some mullars, pounders, beads and sling ball.

The earlier cultural tradition was continued without any perceptible change in period II. Only the advent of iron - technology in this level was the most significant innovation. Most of the shapes in Black and Red wares of period I continued in this period.

Among the minor antiquities, mention may be made of stone mullars, pounders, sharpner, beads of semi - precious stones, terracotta beads, balls and figurines. Eight pieces of iron and few lump of iron slags have been recovered from this level. Among the iron objects, a single piece of sickle constituting a low carbon hyoecutectoid steel may be identified.

The floor levels of rammed earth, post holes and fragments of wattle and daub construction represent their dwellings or courtyard. A fire place in one of the floor level near the entrance is an important discovery of the period.

The report of the Zoological Survey of India on the identification of animal bones include demesticated variety of humped cattle, buffaloes, pig, from period 1. The sixty percent (60%) bone remains of this period is domesticated humped cattle. The bones of Zebu, pig, goat, sheep are also present in later collection.

Soil samples of the habitation deposit of early village farming community at the site contained phosphate, calcium-carbonate, organic carbon, nitrogen etc. The analysis of the soil also suggest that maximum rise of population had been taken place in the mid level of period II. The higher content of some of them suggest increase in human activity and presence of domesticated animal in the habitational area.

A single piece of dating out of seven samples may be accepted which is as follows. (10)

PRL 1191 : 2870 $\pm$ 120 B.P. HTR4 Tr.A_1 Layer : 61.92 mts. Pd : II.

Dihar : The archaeological site of Dihar is situated on the bank of river Dwarakeswar near Visnupur, District : Bankura beside the twin late medieval Siva temple of Saileswar and Shanreswar, built during Malla period of Visnupur. For the reconstruction of the socio - cultural pattern of pre, proto and early historic people of the chhotonagpur plateau region of West Bengal, the site was excavated by the Department of Archaeology, University of Calcutta.

The occupational level at this site revealed mud floors and post - holes. The floors were made of beaten earth, rammed terracota and plastered with lime. The construction of houses or court - yard were simple and occurrence of post - holes has been found in various layers e.g. layer number five (5) and so on. Due to limited scale of excavation, architectural planning of the houses at this site could not be traced.

The microliths discovered from occupational levels are blades, scrapers, thumb - nail scraper, lunates and a few micro cores (Flutted core variety). The raw materials are quartzite, chert, quartz, pebble and other silicious rock - materials, possibly obtained from the bed of Dwarakeswar.

The copper objects sometimes scattered all over the floor level comprised of picks, chisels, with broad and narrow end, scrapers, needles and drills.

Occurrence of bone tools though very few in number probably suggest the replacement of the former by copper technology. The site is devoid of any terracotta object in proto - historic context. Beads of semi - precious stone like agate, felsper, jadite and haematite have been recovered from early historic level.

The occupational level of proto - historic phase has yielded BRW, Cream slipped ware, incised ware beside painted variety of BRW bearing simple carvilinear design on the interior black surface in white chrome. The noteworthy designs are short oblique strokes, dots, dashes parallel horizontal lines. The shapes are carinated bowl, convex sided bowl with a sagger base, channel spouted bowl and bowl with slightly everted rim.

A large settlement is found to have come into existence at Dihar with the advent of copper technology. The river valleys of Dwarakeswar and Damodar was dominated by BRW culture designated as Early Village Farming Culture of this area. It has been assumed that painted and plain variety of BRW probably indicate the existence of two distinct cultural streams. But when they co - existed at the same site & level, they are not distinguishable.

On the basis of excavated materials and evidence of carbon fourteen (C_{14}) or Radio - carbon dating, it is almost certain that by about 1000 B.C., the BRW people of Dihar settled on the older alluvium tract, watered by the Dwarakeswar. (11)

Mahishdal : The site is situated on the bank of Kopai near Prantik Rly. station in the district of Birbhum. It was excavated by Archaeological Survey of India, Eastern Circle in 1964 - 65. The earliest period was characterised by copper, stone and bone using village farming community who were acquainted with the manufacturing of wheel made pottery like BRW, Red ware, Black slipped ware. The next period had witnessed the introduction of Iron. The copper objects include bangle, ring and a single piece of copper axe with broad cutting edge.

The inhabitants of Mahisdal were also acquainted with the manufacturing of microliths like scraper, point etc and bone tools like pin, ornaments like decorated comb, beads of terracotta and semi precious stones and a terracotta phallic emblem.

The walls of the houses were the out come of mud and nodules, plastered with lime. The discovery of charred rice from the floors of Period I indicate it's probale use as a granery or kitchen.

Apart from the manufacturing of various objects, serving daily necessity, the people of Mahishdal prepared wheel turned pottery like BRW, Red ware, Black slipped ware for vessel, bowl, basin, and spouted bowl.

A carbon fourteen (C-14) analysis of the excavated charred rice suggest a date of 1000 B.C. for period I. The beginning of this period was attested by other C-14 dating as Circa. 1485 B.C. while Circa. 795 B.C. to Circa 585 B.C. for period II. (12)

Mogulmari, Dantan : Purva - Medinipur : The Department of Archaeology, University of Calcutta excavated the site of Mogulmari, Dantan during 2003 - 2004. The objectives of the excavation is to establish the cultural sequence and settlement system and the identification of ancient DANDABHUKTI. Two seperate area viz Structural mound (Mgm 1) and Settlement mound (Mgm 2) as revealed by the explorations were excavated.

Apart from iron nail, pottery, terracotta and brick structure, Mgm 2 has yielded seven layers representing two broad cultural phases viz. chalcolithic (BRW - culture) - layers 2 & 3 ; and early medieval layers 5 and 6, with a sterile layer number 4 in between. The proto - historic inhabitants of the site were acquainted with the use of BRW, RW, Black on red ware. The shapes in major cases are Bowls, Basins and cooking vessels (Handi). (13)

Excavation at Mangalkot, Bardhaman : The archaeological site of Mangalkot is situated on the right bank of Kunoor river in the Katwa subdivision of Bardhaman District,West Bengal. It is 35 kms. North - East from Bardhaman Sadar town and 19 kms east of Gushkara Rly. station.

The site is characterised by the older alluvium, inters-persed with flat alluvium stretches of the Gangetic valley. The river Kunoor flows along the western margins and then meets Ajay. After flowing a distance of about 12 kms towards east, they finally disgorge into the main stream at Bhagirathi in Katwa.

The present village of Mangalkot is placed right on the ancient mound, measuring roughly four square miles North - South and East - West and occupies the total area of habitation in ancient time. The excavated mound rises 14 to 15 mts above the surrounding agricultural land mass.

The excavation at the sites envisages the existence of six - phases of which bottom phases belongs to BRW culture. A close observation of the bone tools, excavated from period I and II delineates a clear truth that the early village farmers of Mangalkot used tools of bones more often than stone. On the basis of finished, unfinished tools and raw materials unearthed from each layers, it seems that almost every house - hold prepared its own tools, mainly comprised of points, daggers arrow heads, blades and awls. Use of iron has been noticed right from the bottom level, though on a restricted scale. The use of copper was very much limited ; apart from fish hook, it was used primarily for making ornaments.

The structural remains of Mangalkot are made of bamboo and leaf or straw - like material. The walls are made of read screens, plastered with mud ; the floors in some cases are made with bedding of gravels and cobbles, rammed in hard silty clay.

The chronology of BRW phase at Mangalkot seems to have ranged from Circa 1200 B.C. to Circa 600 B.C. on the basis of a radio carbon dating. The C-14 analysis undertaken at the Physical Research laboratory, Ahmedabad on the charcoal samples available from the level of BRW phase (MGT - 2, A1, layer : 7). The analysis has given a date as 2870 +150 B.P. which correspondence to 940 B.C.

Apart from BRW, with or without painting, many other varieties of red slipped ware, lustrous red ware, chocolate red ware, dull red ware, black slipped ware, a kind of brown, black polished ware, cream slipped ware and a few hand made ill fired coarse grey and brown red ware has been noticed in period I. The noteworthy shapes are Cooking vessels, Bowls, Globular vessels, Vases, Basins speaks in favour of utiliterian types. Besides these types, fragments of Bowl on stand and Dish on stand in both BRW and Black slipped ware including helmet shaped Vase with abruptly extended rims have been found in an appreciable number.

Period II is characterised by the occurrence of some new pottery types like grey, black - slipped, red - slipped, mat red and BRW with the latter occurring in lesser quantity. The miniature deep bowl of thin walled fine textured red coloured sherd with incurved rim is worth mentioning as a special ceramic type of this time.

The earliest inhabitants of Mangalkot seemed to have depended on the tools like points, pin, awls, swords, knife, scraper, blades, arrowheads made of splintered bones and antler. The bone types are varied ranging from antler to tortoise shell, besides bones of domesticated animals, birds, tortoise and fish. Some of the pieces show a clear chiselled mark indicating that metal implements have been used in manufcturing tools. Stone tools are conspicuously absent. Indeed, except two pieces of microliths, Mangalkot did not provide evidence of stone tools during the BRW - phase and transitional period.

Copper, though noticed from very begining, found mostly for making personal adornments. These include rings and bangles. A single piece of fish - hook proved the evidence of the use of copper for making tool. But iron was used sporadically at this site from the beginning of BRW phase. At the upper layers of period II, iron was used for manufacturing sickle, hoe, point etc. Rate of metal consumption also prove that iron had an important bearing on the life and economy of the people of Mangalkot from very ancient time.

Apart from beads of semi - precious stone and terracotta, terracotta figurines of human being and a bull consist the kit of antiquity. Period I reveals only a few specimens of human figurines, representing an ageless type of object exhibiting a highly generalised modelling. Of these, one designed with applique probably associated with the Mother goddess cult, though there has not been any special attempt to delineate the figure as female. Period II of Mangalkot has yielded a large number of stylised animal forms, net sinkers, spindle - whorls, figurines including bust of a female. All the terracotta objects of period I and II are handmade.

The early village farming community of Mangalkot using BRW - were essentially agriculturist, yet one of the main item of their food consisted of species like carp, fish and tortoise. A profuse number of bones of hog-deer and swamp deer found from the site strongly suggest that these were hunted primarily for the flesh. The antlers were used for making bone tools. The remains of domesticated cattle and pig are also profuse in number.

The excavated evidence of Mangalkot indicate the existence of an well established agricultural life without any pre-historic base. Though some hand made coarse pottery of gritty nature occured at the basal level along with BRW and other ceramics, yet no cultural break has been noticed between the earlier hunter - gatherers and BRW phase. Remains of wheel made pottery, copper objects, bone tools, bone remains of consumed animals, beads of semi precious stone, terracotta objects, microliths, neoliths, remains of thatched hut and miscellaneous object clearly suggest an inter regional contact.

The evidence of iron found from the basal level of Mangalkot suggest that any reason connected with the development of the BRW phase of these early village farmers, was the use of iron technology beside the bone tools and limited use of copper. The site is also claiming that it is the only site in West Bengal which provided the existence of a transitional phase between the BRW and Early historic period. Moreover these people gradually developed a good contact with the north Indian socio-economic political waves with an idea of forming first urban settlement in this part of West Bengal during Mauryan period. (14)

Nanur, Birbhum : The site was excavated by Ashutosh Art Gallery, Calcutta University in 1945. But the excavation did not confirm the existence of BRW culture as well as the archaeological importance of the mound. It was reexcavated by the Archaeological Survey of India, Eastern Circle in the year of 1967 - 68.

The excavation has proved the habitation deposits of two periods. The former period is characterised by early village farming settlers while the latter by iron users who achieved higher technology of iron smelting for manufacturing of agricultural tool as well as implements like sword, dagger, arrow head, spear head etc.

The ceramics of earlier phase including BRW, Red ware bears a good amount of similarity with the same type of pottery, excavated from other sites of Birbhum. Beside ceramic assemblage microliths, iron implements, stone, bone and terracotta beads are also bear similarity with antiquities recovered from other sites of the District. (15)

Salkhana / Haraipur. (Yakher Danga) : Birbhum : The site is situated on the bank of Mayurakshi near Purandarpur on Suri - Santhia Highway. It was excavated by Archaeiological Survey of India, Eastern Circle, during the field session of 1967 - 68.

Salkhana or Haraipur exhibited a double cultural habitation envisaging early village farmers and iron users. Beside BRW and Grey ware, the excavation has revealed ten skeletons belonging to ten individuals who died after enjoying a short tenure of life span, suggesting once again it's use as a burial ground.

The heads are oriented to north. But the famous site of Pandurajar Dhibi envisages a different feature in respect of the orientation of the dead body. The heads of the latter site were oriented towards east and as such it may be assumed that the early village farmers, resided on the either side of Ajay river (North & South) buried their dead bodies in two different ways. (16)

Tulshipur : Bankura : The site is situated below the confluence of the rivers Kasai and Kumari in the District of Bankura.

A small scale excavation was conducted jointly by the Archaeological Survey of India, Eastern Circle and Sydney University, Australia. The aim of the excavation is to form an idea about the nature of the BRW - phase and early iron age cultures of the region and to obtain a stratified sequence from Pre-historic time to early historic period.

The excavation revealed three main phases of which the first two showed a continuous development. The characteristics of each phases are as follows.

The earliest phase was represented by some floors & pits and a gritty red slipped, BRW and micaceous ware. In the next phase, black polished pottery, a few gritty red slipped wares and some BRW sherds were found. Iron was found in both the phases. The last phase was characterised by a bright red ware occurring in recent sand which covered much of the site to a depth of about 50 cms. (17)

Tamluk, Purva Medinipur : Tamluk, ancient Tamralipta was subjected to excavation since 1940 by Eastern Circle, Archaeological Survey of India. It was reexcavated in 1955. The excavation report of 1940 and 1955 does not mention the existence of the habitation of EVFC at the site. The exploration by D A & M, Govt. of West Bengal at the site in the year of 1965, 1968 and 1970 has yielded evidence of chalcolithic habitation. The site was excavated once again by the Archaeological Survey of India, Eastern Circle in 1973 - 74.

The excavation during 1973 - 74 has revealed the occurrence of early historic evidence along with the evidence of Black and Red ware from lower levels. The probe during this time has proved the existence of four phases. The first two phases are Pre-metallic and next two phases are metallic. The earliest phase had witnessed the occurrence of microliths, polished implements and bone tools beside BRW, RW, BPW. The RW was sometimes painted in black chrome envisaging geometric motifs while in case of black and red ware, they were painted in white chrome on the black inner surface. (18)

Pakhanna : The site is situated above the right bank of river Damodar. It is identified with ancient city of Pushkarna / Pushkalavati, the capital of king Chandravarman referred to in the Susunia Rock inscription of Gupta period.

The aim of the excavation is to determine the nature and character of cultural assemblages particularly from the period of transaction from BRW - Early historical period at the habitation deposit of the site. Discovery of an urn burial at the mound of Kalyanpur during the course of earlier excavation requires further investigation on the other parts of the site confirm it's use and other technical aspect.

The site was subjected to excavation under the supervision of the Department of Archaeology, University of Calcutta. The twin mound of the site has revealed almost similar deposition as revealed during the course of excavation. They are Pakhanna I ((Bhairavdanga mound) and Pakhanna II (Kalyanpur mound).

The most important discovery of Pakhanna is the evidence of iron smelting activities in six successive levels at PKN : 1 (Bhairabdanga). The evidences are found in the form of hearths, charcoal, ash, iron implements, potsherds etc. At the lowest level, terracotta basin for storage of water has also been found attached to the hearth. These complexes represent secondary type of iron smelting activities at the area. The important iron objects are chisel, arrowhead, nail etc. Beads of banded agate and carnelian were discovered. The ceramic industry is rich in Black and Red ware, as the diagnostic type. The pottery of this phase consists of BRW, Black ware, Red ware, Buff ware, Chocolate ware etc.

At PKN : 2, three cultural periods viz Post Gupta, Gupta and Kushana were found. In Post Gupta phase, ceramic types consists of Red ware, Black ware and Buff ware. The most characteristic type is vessel with knife edge variety. Two terracotta figurines excavated from the site wearing 3-tiered headgear, recalling similar type from South Bengal. Thick and massive storage jars with conical base, shallow dishes, bowls, basins, footed cups, terracotta animal figures and other antiquities have also been discovered.

Tools made of splintered bone and arrowhead, sometime other types of cut - bones have been recovered from Bhairavdanga. (19)

In the foregoing pages, we have surveyed the basic material remains excavated from the various sites of West Bengal, except Pandurajar Dhibi as it require a seperate chapter for detailed analysis. The survey aimed at it's general content associated with rise and growth of village settlements in this part of India.

The excavation has revealed that the early village farmers of West Bengal lived in huts having red screened and mud plastered wall and floors of beaten moorum or lime plastered in it's initial stages. The lime plastered gobri floors noticed frequently. Sometimes post holes were noticed in these floors probably for raising huts or tying the ropes of domesticated animals, who supplied food articles in the form of meat and other substances. The floor levels of some sites were prepared by rammed earth, post holes and fragment of wattle and daub. Some times fire places were noticed near the entrance. Discovery of charred rice from the floors of Pandurajar Dhibi, Mahishdal indicate it's probable use as a granery and kitchen. Hearths were also noticed in various sites. A couple of open variety " Hearths " approximately 50 cms in diameter, may be stated here in this context from the excavated sites of Bharatpur, in the succeeding habitational layers.

While discussing the over all strategy, reflecting through structural remains, the excavation at Bahiri, Mangalkot and Pakhanna, specified the nature of domestic area and immediate closing area including the courtyard. The excavation in the year 2002 - 2003 at the mound of Bhairavdanga in Pakhanna has yielded extended floor to be treated as courtyard, where as the inner part of habitation was covered with the place for storing on industrial purpose (Potter's hearth or metal working).

Similarly Chakrabarti, while discussing the settlement complex of Bahiri, also specify the hearth and it's associated courtyard. The village society of BRW period certainly crystalize sedantery life style by the recognition of the utilization of space and its function. We have very limited data from Bharatpur, Dihar, Hatikhera and Mahishdal. But Mangalkot may be visualized in terms of habitational set up and their various ways of activities.

Our argument related to the utilisation of space and availability of structural remains, recorded from the excavated site, could be treated according to their hierarchial status. As a result of this, we can trace the definition of different categories of villagers and their relationship with structural activity during the period. The habitation complex of a self sufficient farmer with singularly agrarian base, minor farmer having seasonal farming, the villagers associated with other kind of production in non-agrarian set up, specially the habitation of potter, metalsmith and other categories of producers should be evident in our structural material. Unfortunately the excavators failed to trace the speification of the entire BRW phase (as interpreted in different writtings), always referred passing references to the hierarchial order of such settlement complex. In this context, it is to be mention that the daily labourers or the marginal class of BRW society never interpreted with their habitational complex. The house of fisherman community in the Black and Red ware phase along the bank of the river certainly influenced the dimension of contemporary structural complex. But unfortunately the report concerning such activity never highlighted so far, where as, the appearance of bone tools, metal slag and other productive items closely associated with different producers could be treated in a meaningful way in our recorded structural remains.

Chakrabarti categorically mention the workshop related to metal work and pottery manufacturing. If we follow the report of Chakrabarti on Bahiri, we may found the settlement activity in terms of mixed producer i.e., a potter was associated with metal work. Do we agree with this economy or is it a confusion between the two ? We have some parallel data coming from Hatikhera. There also the same question arises about the scientific characterisation of the settlement. A poor village like Dihar had limited space for agrarian base. It is quite evident that the people of Dihar settled over the mound, atleast certain period of time in Black and Red ware phase with non-agrarian economy. Their strategy related to fishing, harvesting or other wise, also made necessary impact on the habitation context.

It is very difficult to make a comparison within the BRW sites of our region, because the anomoly existed regarding the nature of excavation and information about the general character of BRW site and their relationship with the different aspect of life and society during BRW phase. There are several kinds of similarity existed in a material culture. The homogeneous village society could also be realised with reference to evidence that we have. The subsistance pattern, the growth of village society in the context of their structural complex of habitational context, ceramic industry, metal technology, technology involved with their craftsmanship, altogether is in a very complex character. Still they are lagging behind in respect of more information to elaborate BRW habitation pattern. However, a close scrutiny resulted in the discovery of some relevent issue related to the evolution of culture including the extension of courtyard, the spatial classification of a total activity areas, if not the other. The housing pattern since the development of daub - wattle complexes, precisely speaking about a villager's accomodation which envisages a place for living area, the places of cooking, pottery manufacturing and the other open space left for domesticated animals. It is also interesting to assume that harvesting and processing of food also require a space allotted by the BRW people. Similarly we have a limited number of date to make a comparison of subsistance pattern dominated the day to day dietary system of BRW phase. Innovation of new technology, the inclination of the use of metal and the departation of earlier obsolate technology also evident in our study materials. In this context, it is worth mentioning that the central and western Indian sites of early village farming period received special attention in the Archaeology of Deccan Collage, Pune. Davalikar, precisely described the art activity of Inamgaon area and it's association with social stratification. Similarly Basant Sindhe also highlighted Balathal specimens in the context of Art & Archaeology of the Aharian Rajasthan.

The major - minor antiquities associated with BRW phase reported from our study area may help us to reconstruct the coherent picture of these early village farmers of West Bengal. Unfortunately our limitation to extend our knowledge about this culture may constrain us to elaborate more.

Notes & References

1. Shyam Chand Mukherji : Chalcolithic image of West Bengal with special reference to Pandurajar Dhibi. Indian Museum Bulletin, Number : 2. 1967. Page : 36.
2. Ibid, Page - 37.
3. H.N.Singh : History and Archaeology of Black and Red ware (Chalcolithic period), 1982, Page : 3 to 49.
4. D.K. Chakrabarti & others : Index of Black and Red ware sites in West Bengal, South Asian Studies, Vol - 9, Page : 123.
5. Ibid, Page : 123 - 135.
6. Indian Archaeology 1974 - 75 : A review. Page : 51.
7. Shyam Chand Mukherji : Excavation at Baneswardanga, District : Bardhaman. Pratna samiksha : Vol - 2 & 3. Page : 80 - 143. 1993 - 94.
8. D.K. Chakrabarti & J.Hassan :Sequence of Bahiri, District Birbhum, West Bengal.
   Man and Environment, 1982 Page 111-149
9. NEWS LETTER : Centre for Archaeological Studies andtraining Eastern India, November : 2003,No-8. Page:14.
10. Indian Archaeology 1986 - 87. A Review. Page : 94, 95.
11. A.C. Pal : Dihar A Chalcolithic Site, Pratna Samiksha, Volume : 1, Page : 101 - 103, 1992.
12. Indian Archaeology 1963 - 64 A Review. Page 59, 60.

12a. Indian Archaeology 1964 -65 A Review. Page : 7, 8, 9.

13. NEWS LETTER : Centre for Archaeological studies and Training, Eastern India, November - 2004, No. 9, Page : 13.
14. Amita Ray and : Excavation at Mangalkot, Samir Kr Mukherjee Pratna Samiksha, Vol : 1, Page - 107-134.

15. Chakrabarti D.K. and others : An Archaeological Reconnassane in Birbhum, Puratattva : 10, Page : 25 - 32.

16. Indian Archaeology 1964-65. A Review. Page : 46.

17. Indian Archaeology 1967-68. A Review. Page : 49-50.

18. Indian Archaeology 1973-74. A Review. Page : 51.

19. NEWS LETTER : Centre for Archaeological Studies and Training, Eastern India, November 2003, No : 8, Page : 13.

3

PANDURAJAR DHIBI AND IT'S ENVIRONMENT

An understanding of the Protohistoric[5] environmental mosaic of Pandurajar Dhibi and it's surroundings is a key to define the distribution of environmental zone in the past. It may also help us to detect the major natural and human resources associated with the contemporary E.V.F. culture of Pandurajar Dhibi. A knowledge of the seasonal and spatial distribution of these features, is a basic factor to the re-construction of the past ecology of Pre and Proto historic time.

The environmental[6] diversity of this area is derived from it's geographical position in the past. In bridging chhotonagpur plateau, the coastal corridor that skirts the gangetic basin has at various time, being colonised by biotic community indegenous to each of the area. The marked topographical variation and natural resources, has also been acted to create environmental refuse of the earlier period.

As a consequence of these geographic, topographic and other related factors, this part of West Bengal presently enjoyed a remarkable environmental set up where forest, arable lands, fertile plains, uneven valleys found in close proximity.[7] But the distribution of major biotic communities are easily altered by slight change in precipitation and temperature patterns. The site Pandurajar Dhibi with the total ecological set up of Bardhaman would also appeared to have been a region of considerable environmental diversity and sensibility to change the climate through out the pleistocene period, gradually merged with Holocene environment. In the following pages, we have tried to explain certain study materials for rendering a coherent picture about the potentiality of the region to give birth of a village community through farming economy.

The environmental condition including the entire ecological set up is certainly different or less known with that of the modern days. However, a report incorporating the environmental data by and large depend on the investigation of geological data and present day environment of the entire landscape including the geographical setting that we observe in the districts of Bardhaman and it's adjoining areas like Birbhum and Bankura.

The environment of Pandurajar Dhibi is synonymous with that of lower gangetic delta. The landscape characterised by flood plains of Bhagarathi basin along with it's tributories like Mayurakshi, Kunoor, Ajay, Damodar and even Dwarakeswar witnessed the plain land, essentially fertile, bearing the potentiality for any kind of cultivation of crops, particularly rice. On the other hand, the undulating landscape of the fringe area of chhotonagpur extension not only render the source of metal, mineral and timber but also harbour a large scale population in the genes group including the tribal, caste and subcaste. The geographical setting in and around Pandurajar Dhibi helped the original inhabitants of the site for the begining and growth of a well determinestic, resource based village farming culture.

Metal and mineral resources played a significant role for the development of village economy in and around Pandurajar Dhibi.[8]

The region has two broad geomorphological characters. The Bhagirathi Hugli basin and the area curved by eastern extension of chhotonagpur plateau is essentially the territory more close to the environment and ecological set up of Pandurajar Dhibi in broad sense. Darjeeling is the main copper bearing district in West Bengal. But it has been also noticed in the districts of Bankura, Purulia, and Paschim - Medinipur. There are altogether ten copper bearing localities in Darjeeling while Tamkhum and Chhedapahar in Bankura shows an evidence of workings and Chhedapahar mines are known to have been extracted since Fifth-Sixth Centuries A. D. Some copper has been reported from Makarbula and Hijli in Purva-Medinipur. At Chirugura in Purulia, thin veinlets of chalcopyrite and Pyrite have been noted in the Beldih Shear zone.

Two types of iron ores namely clay iron stones of the middle Damudas and laterite ores of the eastern part of the Raniganj coalfield area are an important source of iron from time immorial.[1]

The Archaeological work at Kankrajhore and Dhuliapur in the Paschim - Medinipur district revealed that the neolithic culture was succeeded directly by iron age culture[2]. At Mahishdal on the bank of Kopi in West Bengal and Barudih on the bank of Sanjay, Bihar iron is found associated with microliths and Neolithic tools. The dates in both cases are 1000 B. C. The tool types from Pandurajar Dhibi, Mahisdal Chirand, Barudih etc suggest a well developed and extensive iron industry in the column of BRW. There were important production centres for apply of iron objects and / or bloom to the valley in chhotonagpur plateau[3].

The persistent and non persistent character of behavioural pattern of mankind or a particular Population Structure, could be traced with the help of an ethnological approach.

The people living in the rooms of grass leaves, reeds or bamboos, mud or unburnt bricks occupied the major habitation since time immemorial.

Different categories of social groups including service class constitute the major number of population in rural sector.[10] Their social status depends on the nature of subsistance economy and pattern. The sub - caste and caste beside tribal group occupy a major number in & around the area of our present discussion. A gross classificationn of such distribution of population suggest the existence of agrarian and non-agrarian communities at present, including Milk man, Farmer, Fisherman, Blacksmith, Goldsmith and Potter. Apart from this, the person connected with the profession of washing and dying of cloth, Weaver, Cobler beside service class like Butler, Soldier, Kaviraj, Traders and labourers and tribal elements during modern times on the South-West part of Pandurajar Dhibi. The latter constitute of Santhal, Kora, Oraon, Munda, Mahalis etc suggest a particular type of profession around the region. But it's relationship with existing class structure may not be similar to that of the past. However, there are some groups who display their age-old profession including traditional economy, owing to society. All these social demography is essential to a broad spectrum of house hold economy beside the labour forces of early village farming economy, if not, the so called semi-urbanised iron using society.

The aforesaid study, throw some light on their role for the procurement of day to day community, including the supply of metal, mineral, timber beside fishing and agricultural activities.

The presence of tribal groups[11] in and around Pandurajar Dhibi, hinted towards the procurement of timber and other forest product. The cultural and symbiotic relationship between agrarian set up and forest clad visualise till today is an indication of the supply of such materials to their activity, to accelerate the bondage between the population. Similarly for the procurement of metal and mineral, the different occupational group of ore bearing area, might have involve slag smelting techniques. They are different from the sites like Pandurajar Dhibi, Bahiri, Dihar, Kankrajhore in West Bengal and Barudih in Singhbhum, Bihar.[4]

The area under present discussion experienced the rise and growth of a particular mankind with their every aspect for giving birth of a rural society with the help of a series of changes from hunting / gathering stage to developed village farming society. It is a transitional zone between chhotonagpur plateau and the Ganga - Brahmaputra alluvial plain and valley plains. The region envisages different types of soils in different topographical, biological conditions. These soils are reddish colour medium to coarse in texture, acidic in reaction, low in nitrogen, calcium, phosphate and other plant nutrients.[11] Water holding capacity of these soils increase with the depth in clay proportions. The area is very much rich in terms of mineral production.

The climate of the region[12] hardly differs from the overall mesothermal climatic pattern. The present Gangetic monsoon climate in the south-eastern parts of the area is characterised by moderate temperature with cold weather. The other characteristics is the prevalance of high relative humidity through out the year. The variation of rain fall from year to year is not large. This number varies from sixty (60) at Mangalkot to seventy-eight (78) at the area of our discussion. On an average, there are seventy (70) rainy days in a year.

Changing pattern of economy for survival, different routes of migration and even natural calamities and other consequences adversely effected to the population structure of this region from time immemorial. The study of population [10] and their distribution has no relevance to know the age old class structure and apply them to the early village farming community of Pandurajar Dhibi. The most active group of all these population structure was potter as suggested by the present potters village, which once again domonstrate that they were the direct ancestor of early village potters' community of Pandurajar Dhibi. Beside this, the presence of weaving, fishing, skin / leather working classes have played an important role for the development of village settlement at Pandurajar Dhibi during middle of the 2nd. m.m. B.C. The excavated material from the site also tend to show that fishing, hunting, pastoralism beside agriculture constitute all these population structure and their close relationship with the crystalisation of village society.

Notes & References

1. Pranab K Chattopadhyay, Basic Principles and Modern Techniques in the studies of Archaeo - materials in Eastern India, Science in Archaeology and Archaeo materials, Edited by Arun Kr Biswas, Page : 319 & 320.
2. Ibid : Page : 325 to 327.
3. Ibid : Page : 325.
4. Indian Archaeology 1982 - 1983 A Review. Page : 104.
5. West Bengal District Gazetters : Bardhaman, Page : 1 - 5.
6. Ibid : Page 6 to 10.
7. Ibid : Page 11 to 29.
8. Ibid : Page 30 to 43.
9. ibid : Page 29 to 43.
10. Ibid : Page 100 to 159.
11. Ibid : Page 134 to 146.
12. Ibid : Page 49 to 60.
13. Ibid : Page 100 to 159.

4

HISTORY OF EXCAVATION AND NATURE OF EXCAVATED MATERIALS : PANDURAJAR DHIBI, BARDHAMAN, WEST BENGAL

Inspired by the discovery of BRW site at Sonpur and some other sites of Bihar and Jharkhand under the leadership of B.P. Sinha, Directorate of Archaeology & Museum, Government of West Bengal carried out exploration in the districts of Bankura, Birbhum & Burdwan under the leadership of Paresh Chandra Dasgupta, resulted the subsequent discovery of Pre and Proto- historic sites. However, it was summer of 1961, when Dasgupta was able to pick sizeable collection of BRW from the site of Pandurajar Dhibi. He also visited the adjascent area of Pandurajar Dhibi i.e. Panduk & Dinanathpur near the Bazar complex.

It was possibly an opportunity of Dasgupta when his co- investigator D. K. Chakaraborti and Dr. S. C. Mukherji stuck with the collection of BRW and microlithic tools along with core materials. Dasgupta's writing categorically stated that he was fully convinced with the material and it's relationship with the early village farming community of the site. After a re-visit at the site during latter half of the year 1961, Dasgupta concentrated to execute some research work on the early village farmers of the area. With this aim in mind, he confined himself to record more data and tried to remove the mystry of the site and it's assemblage. He procured suggestions of various scholars including Professor H. D. Sankalia of Deccan College, Pune to justify his future decision of excavation. While attending the Centinary celebration of Archaeological Survey of India at New Delhi in 1961, Dasgupta met with Professor Sankalia for making him aware about the importance of the site. Moreover, he put forward a note about his discovery to the scholars in the gathering. The centinary conference declared the site Pandurajar Dhibi as an early habitation of Bengal Village farmers. It was a great moment for Dasgupta because he travelled a long uneven path before the discovery of Pandu Rajar Dhibi and subsequent recognition.

Source Material

Excavation at the site has resulted a good number of publication about the materials and other aspects of Pandurajar Dhibi. Beside the excavation report, published by the excavator, the other publication including some personal research work of different scholars like Deb Kumar Chakrabarti, Dr. Shyam Chand Mukherji, Sudhin Dey, Professor Amita Roy, Dr. Asok Datta, Professor Diilip Kr. Chakrabarti, Dr. R. K. Chattopadhyay, etc. enrich our analysis. Apart from this, there are some report on botanical, metal and bone sample analysis collected from the site in the form of scientific excavation, by Dr. Manomoy Ghosh, Dr. Utpal Saha and Dr. Pranab Kr. Chattopadhyay.

For the critical reference to the site and discovery, one could depend on the summary work of Dilip K. Chakrabarti and his associates. It is worth mentioning that we can find the general observation on Pandurajar Dhibi in the writing of different archaeologist & scholars like Professor A. Roy, Professor A. Pal, Dr. A. Datta, F. R. Alchin and B. Alchin, D. P. Agarwal, Amalananda Ghosh, Asok K. Ghosh, H. N. Singh, K. M. Srivastava, H. D. Sankalia and others including the result of excavation and analysis of finding of Pandurajar Dhibi in their respective works. Vertually one can easily find the reference to Pandurajar Dhibi in any archaeological book of India having a proto-historic section.

The primary source as well as secondary sources having utilised in the present assessment about the site and antiquity. In turn the above academic exercise, may helpful for going through the analysis of data with a more scientific mind. Though built - in - problem in the excavation report and published data may create anomaly and confusion, we generally tried to remove such problem in liberal and academic way. Argument and counter argument sometimes generated more critical knowledge for the persuation of liberal approach and assessment, our finding along with the contemporay literature related to our topic particularly.

The development of research on Eastern Indian Archaeology in general and West Bengal in particular is throughly understandable in the work of Dilip K. Chakrabarti. The contribution of Paresh Chandra Dasgupta on Proto historic parts of West Bengal had received a very strong opinion formulated by Chakrabarti. He has discussed aims and objectives of P. C. Dasgupta related to discovery of BRW - site. He also summarised the new objectives of the excavator before the probe at Pandurajar Dhibi. Though Chakrabarti is not satisfied with the result of excavation, given enough credit to Dasgupta for high-lighting his major ambition.

Beside the discovery of Pandurajar Dhibi, Dasgupta dotted successfully some other BRW site in the map of West Bengal. His vision was to show the extension of Ganga Valley

Culture upto lower Gangetic delta. And in this understanding, we are quite successful to trace the same. While excavating Bahiri at Birbhum, Chakrabarti also made essential comparison between the multi dimensional activity of Bahiri and Pandurajar Dhibi. Though he expressed disappointment on published report in several occassion, yet his discussion on Dasgupta's achievement extended to admit and acknowledge the discovery of Pandurajar Dhibi in different manner and quite clarity. We may assume that he was virtually unaware with the analytical device of the report rather than objective. So the unfortunate part may be treated as the lack of necessary infrastructure, the paucity of comperative material and the general perspective of Bengal Archaeology. As a result we are confrontred by some confusing decision. Scholarly acceptance of the site could be recorded in various ways including the visit of H. D. Sankalia at Pandurajar Dhibi and white press citation.

The name Pandurajar Dhibi derives from a local legend based on a certain king, named Pandu whose palace is said to have been buried in the core of the main mound. The region finds it's place in the Jaina text as Paniyabhum or Panitabhum in connection with Mahavir's itinerary to Vajrabhumi in Radha / Ladha in West Bengal as early as 6th Century B. C. which once again suggest internal trade. The Rigvedic word Pani, being sometimes explained as traders. Though the argument has lots of limitation in the context of history and other supporting records.

The varied topography of West Bengal, including fertile river banks, broken coasts as well as arid tracts with galleries of hills, and patches of dense forests of SAL inspired us about the existence of a proto historic culture in this part of West Bengal. The excavation at Pandurajar Dhibi has been launched by the Directorate of Archaeology & Museums, W. B. with an objective of establishing the evidences related with the emergence of early village farming communities, within the context of said topography. The antiquities discovered from the site proved about the existence of such an inhabitants who settled here for the time during protohistoric phase. The strange affinities between the finding of sites and those from Central India and Rajasthan also dated the former time bracket ranging from C. 2nd Millenium B. C.

As a result of this discovery, attention of experts were drawn. The auspicious visit of Dr. H. D. Sankalia, Director of Deccan College, Poona, to the site in the month of January, 1962 recognised Pandurajar Dhibi as an outstanding protohistoric habitation deposit in Ajay Valley. It was after the visit of Professor Sankalia, preparation of an excavation was in process.

The excavation at Pandurajar Dhibi was conducted under the leadership of Paresh Chandra Dasgupta and assisted by Deb Kumar Chakrabarti and Dr. Shyam Chand Mukherji.

Sarbasree E. D. Sampson, Pramanath Malakar, Pratul Sen, Anil Karmakar, Nepal Chandra Bhattacharya, Bhabatosh Majumdar, Kanak Kanti Majumdar, Ram Narayan Pal and Ranjit Sen were the other members who did the job of survey, digging, chemical preservation, recording and photography during the course of excavation at Pandurajar Dhibi.

The first phase of excavation was carried out in the spring of 1962. Altogether four trenches were dug, one on the northern slope of the main mound (RDB I : 36' x 10'), one on it's southern foot (RDB III : 15' x 9'), one one the crest of the mound (RDB IV : 24' x 12') and the fourth trench was located to the east of the mound (RDB II : 15' x 10'). Amongst the excavated trenches, RDB I and RDB IV offered a continuous sequences from the dawn of Proto history.

The C_{14} analysis of the charcoal samples excavated from the site was conducted by Dr. Shyamadas Chatterjee, Head of the Department of Physics, Jadavpur University, Kolkata and Physical Research Laboratory, Navarangapura, Ahmedabad.

The first phase of excavation had witnessed that the habitation in period I has penerated into mottled red silt and bears evidences of an agricultural people, making ill fired, hand made crude and pale red grey or black ware of thick fabric showing impressions of paddy husk in the section.

Period II has revealed the introduction of a developed culture by a new group of people who were more advanced and civilised than the earlier inhabitants. They were responsible for incorporating lime plastered smooth floor. Apart from this, occurance of wheel made BRW and lustrous Red Ware (painted in black chrome) marked a clear demarcation regarding the existence of a developed agricultural community in comparison with the earlier.

The layers of period III has revealed the existence of lime plastered floor, studded with a double row of terracotta ovens, elliptical or circular in shape, washed with lime and built at right angles to each other. They were filled with cinders and bone.

The occurence of painted and plain BRW and RW with various shapes and sizes have been noticed beside beads of semi- precious stone and a copper point. The evidence of extensive conflagration at the upper level of this period indicated the reason behind the end of period III.

Same trenches were subject to excavation in the next season and occupation of the site comprised of four cultural periods as against five, determined last year. The excavation in 1962 - 63 threw a welcome light on burial practices. Three periods were assignable to the habitational deposit of early village farmers of Pandurajar Dhibi namely Period I, II, & III with a time bracket ranging from C. 1600 B.C. to C. 600 B.C.

The habitation area of period I has yielded a fractional burial showing East - West orientation with few pot-sherds (1962-63). The next phase has yielded nine burials of three different types beside the routine occurence of microlithic tools, cores and flakes, copper objects, plain & painted BRW, LRW, and chocolate ware and a single piece of polished celt.

Previous years of excavation has noticed the occurrence of iron arrow head and a ground polished celt beside the fragment of dish in black burnished ware bedecked with an incised decoration, showing a pea hen or crane holding a serpent by it's bill from period

The excavation in 1962 - 63 had also witnessed same assemblage with an ivoroy comb, terracotta mother goddess with pin hole decoration and few iron objects from period III.

The excavation in nine fresh trenches on the north - slope of the central portion of the mound in 1963-64 had shown the evidence of a gap between period I and II. Introduction of iron was made in period III. Beside the usual ceramic assemblage as stated earlier, several clay seals with double axe motif and a couple of terracotta human head also occurred in period III.

The Western part of the mound was excavated during the field season of 1964-65. The excavation has yielded the four fold sequences, beside the evidence of some new aspects of occupation.

Publication

The publication on the materials of Pandurajar Dhibi started from the first season of excavation. The report of excavation had find it's place in the respective volumes of Indian Archaeological Review - A bulletin of the Archaeological Survey of India, ranging from 1961-62 to 1965-66. After this, a brief report about the site appeared in the scene of publication, in the form of a seperate volume under the title, " The Excavation at Pandurajar Dhibi " by Paresh Chandra Dasgupta in November, 1964. A seperate chapter was devoted to " PRAGAITIHASIK BANGLA " (in bengali) about the excavated materials of the site by the same author. Apart from these two books, Dasgupta also published a Brochure entitled as " Exploring Bengal's Past " on the mid way of the work during 1963. The same year had also witnessed the mention about the site in a small volume, entitled as " Archaeological Discovery of West Bengal: A Bulletin of the Directorate of Archaeology, West Bengal, Volume : I. "

Apart from this, various scholars also highlighted different aspect of the excavation in different Journals, Periodicals, and Bulletins. Among them, mention may be made of the analysis of excavated skeletal remains by Anadi Pal and Prabir Gupta in the Bulletin of the Archaeological Survey of India, Volume : XIX, 3 & 4 under the title " Human Skeletal Materials Excavated from Pandurajar Dhibi. " Animal remains and Bone-tools from Pandurajar Dhibi were studied and published by Dr. Manomoy Ghosh & Dr. Utpal Saha, Senior Zoologist, Zoological Survey of India in Pratna Samiksha, Volume : I, 1992 : A Journal of the Directorate of Archaeology & Museums, Department of Information & Cultural Affairs, Government of West Bengal. Another article on the excavation of the site was published in Volume : 2 of Indian Museum Bulletin, 1967, under the title as " Chalcolithic image of West Bengal with special reference to Pandurajar Dhibi " by Dr. Shyam Chand Mukherji, Ex-Deputy Director of Archaeology, West Bengal.

The other significant works were published in the volumes of Man and Environment, South Asian Studies, Puratatva, Pratnatattva of Jahangirnagar University, Dacca, Eastern Anthropologist, Pratna Samiksha and so on by the scholars like, Professor Amita Ray, Professor Dilip K. Chakrabarti, Dr. Asok K. Datta, Dr. Rupendra Kumar Chattopadhyay, Mrs. Madhusri Nag, Dr. Durga Basu and myself. The result and their analysis clearly suggest the existence of a well developed village farming community based on seperate family with their individual huts and courtyards in the column of aggrarian as well as hunting economy.

The geometric and non-geometric paintings on the Black and Red Ware, Red Ware, Chocolate Ware, excavated from Pandurajar Dhibi has been studied by the present author with the title " Chalcolithic painted pottery of Pandurajar Dhibi " in Pratna Samiksha, Volume : I, 1992. The other aspects of the site in brief including pottery, metal & bone objects, burials, beads, had been studied by the present author and subsequently published in " Pratnatattva " - a journal of the Jahangir Nagar University, Dacca, Bangladesh with the title " Pandurajar Dhibi : An Earliest Rural Settlement in West Bengal, India ", in Volume - 8, June - 2002.

A monograph with an introduction from Paresh Chandra Dasgupta was published in 1966, dealing with the Stone Age and Proto-history of West Bengal along with a note on chemical preservation of excavated antiquities. The authors are Deb Kumar Chakrabarti, Dr. Shyam Chand Mukherji and Anil Kumar Karmakar of the Directorate of Archaeology and Museums, Government of West Bengal.

Notes & References

1. P. C. Dasgupta. : Archaeological Discovery in West Bengal, A Bulletin of the Directorate of Archaeology, West Bengal, Volume : 1 Page : 1. 1963.
2. P. C. Dasgupta. : The Excavation At Pandurajar Dhibi - A Bulletin of the Directorate of Archaeology, West Bengal, Volume 2, Page : 11 to 34. 1964.

3. P. C. Dasgupta. : Exploring Bengal's Past, Edited volume, Page : 11 to 22, 1966. Published by the Directorate of Archaeology, West Bengal.

4. S. C. Mukhjerji. : Chalcolithic image of West Bengal with reference to Pandurajar Dhibi, Indian Museum Bulletin, Volume : 2, Page : 36 to 49. 1967.

5. S. C. Mukherji. : An unpublished official report on earlier and later excavation at Pandurajar Dhibi, Burdwan, W. B. Dated to 8.8.1985.

6. Indian Archaeology 1984 - 1985 A Review, Page : 97 & 98.

7. T. Banerjee : Chalcolithic Painted Pottery of Panduraja, Dhibi. Pratna - Samiksha, Volume : 1, Page : 77 to 88, 1992.

8. T. Banerjee : Pandurajar Dhibi : An Earliest Rural, Settlement in West Bengal, India Pratnatatva, A journal of the Department of Archaeology, Jahangirnagar University, Savar, Dhaka, Bangladesh, Volume : VIII, June : 2002, Page : 63 to 72.

9. T. Banerjee : A culture fased on OSTEOKERATIC Artefacts unearthed from Pandurajar Dhibi, Arf Archaeology, and Cultural History of India (U.N. Roy Felicitation Volume) Vol-I, P.P. 257-258, B.R. Publishing Corporation, Delhi, 110052, 2005.

5

STRUCTURAL REMAINS

The present chapter highlighted on the pattern of structural remains used by the makers of BRW phase with special emphasis on the sites of Bihar, Jharkhand and West Bengal. The BRW people enjoyed a multi-dimensional character, attested by the records of Structural Remains discovered so far. Our structural analysis is mainly concentrated on the problems of Floor, Courtyard, Oven and Dumping pit.

The structural activity in South Bihar plain suggest the use of perishable materials like reeds, bamboos with mud-plastered walls. The floors of the houses were of burnt earth. A couple of ash-pits were also found near the floor.[1.] The early village farmers of this part of India laid their first habitation on sand dunes while the contemporary Central Indian village farmers had started their structural activities on the black cotton soil.[2]

There were evidence of a smooth lime plastered floor in a large room from period II at Pandurajar Dhibi[3]. Occurrence of a double row of terracotta oven has been noticed from the same site from period III[4]. The houses at Chirand in period I were circular on plan and were constructed of wild reeds as evidenced by the findings of burnt pieces of mud-plasters bearing reed as well as the impression of bamboos. The existence of 75 cms thick mud wall around the dwelling probably suggest some circular or oblong shape of houses. They were still made of impermanent materials.[5]

The early village farmers of Chirand at period I lived on a floor with depressions and a series of ovens with post-holes[6.] The latter characteristics suggest it's probable use as courtyard. Excavation at Bharatpur, has revealed the presence of a few reed impression burnt clay plasters which once again indicate that the contemporary inhabitants lived in huts in period I. A couple of open hearths also encountered from here.[7] The earliest phase at Bharatpur has been dated to 1435 B. C. on the basis C_{14} analysis.[8]

The evidence of structural remains from Dihar, Bankura has revealed the floors of beaten earth with soiling of rammed terracotta nodules and lime. The presence of re-impressed clay daubs, burnt reed impressed clay plasters and large quantities of charcoal suggest a simple structure, befitted in a rural context.[9]

The floors of period I and II of Mangalkot oconsist of a thin layer of rammed hard brownish earth plastered with cow-dung and kankar, occassionally treated with pottery nodules and lime. Reed matting, plastered with mud was picked up near the excavated floor. Five ovens were also traced in three successive levels, arranged side by side on one common platform. Apart from charcoal, some charred bones were also recovered from the oven. On one of the platforms, few large sized pots in BRW were encountered. The pottery recovered in-situ includes Handi, spouted and carinated vase, helmet shaped bowl and a bowl with flaring rim. The early village farmers of the site using BRW may be dated from 1000 B. C. to 700 B. C.

Excavation at Kotasur, Birbhum has revealed the occupational deposit of 3.60 mts. It was divided into three phases. The upper phase, having a thickness of one and a half meter occupation, bear traces of intensive exploitation of available resouces. Trench KTS I has yielded two phases with baked brick structure. The walls of phase II was a part of room with paved flooring. Several tiles with double perforation and shallow finger pressed channels for passing refuse has been noticed from the same level beside the occurrence of iron nails, The middle phase, having one meter thickness was characterised by silts, sand-streaks and eroded surface. The evidence of water logging due to flood has been noticed during this period.[11]

The excavation at Hatikhera, Birbhum attested the evidence of floor levels of rammed earth, post holes and fragment of wattle daub structures. A couple of fire places from the floor levels of different layers has been recorded from period I. The earlier cultural milieu continues without any perceptible change in period II.[12]

Existence of a deep garbage or ash pit was noticed in the north-eastern section of Trench A and south-eastern section of Trench B at PRD. The re-excavation of 1985 has revealed that there was a fixed point or place for dumping the refuse (it might have been a community or family garbage pit). Peoples of different periods used the same pit, as is evidenced by the nature of materials dumped in different periods from the BRW phase downwards. Some interesting antiquities including pottery have been recovered from these pits. A pit has been found in period - I level in trench B and three pits, superimposing each other belonging to periods I & II in trench C. [13]

The belief after death has been reflected through the burial practices at Pandu Rajar Dhibi. There are altogether three types of burials namely Urn Burial, Extended Burial, and Fractional Burial. A couple of Urn burials from period II has yielded human bones and skull of an adult, probably suggest the prevelance of post-cremation.

Period I and II of Pandurajar Dhibi has yielded Extended burial. The orientation of the dead bodies are towards east-west while in one case, the head was turned to the south.

The third type envisages Fractional burial, recorded within the habitation area. These burials included both adult and children. In one case, the upper part of the skeleton is missing. The heads in all the cases turned towards the east.

The burial practice however, bear a close resemblance with similar one in the Deccan plateau and it's immediate North.[14] The funerary goods include terracotta bowls, beads of copper and agate and a scraper.

The analysis of structural remains in Eastern India during BRW phase, particularly at Pandurajar Dhibi, envisages that the early village farmers of the contemporary period were simple living. In other words, the modern Bengali folk are the ancester of these people. They carried the bones of the dead, probably after an exposure in open air, and buried them within their habitation floor. The reason behind this sort of practice may be related with a belief of bringing happiness and prosperity by the departed soul in their family. The concept of living in a group may existed during this time, but the mode of living has been changed as suggested by the small size of the room, sometimes circular or oblong. These rooms may serve the individual dwelling of seperate family, probably consisted of an adult male & female with their children.[15]

The walls and roofs of the houses and courtyards of these people indicate their impermanent nature. The materials used for the construction also throws a sufficient light on a particular aspect of contemporary flora. Though the evidence of walls have been noticed in some excavated trenches of Eastern India, the occurrence of post- holes may indicate the probable existence of courtyard. The supporting post of the roof of these courtyards may serve the purpose of tying the ropes of domesticated animals. The materials used during the construction of floors were mainly kankar, nodule and potsherds while the finishing touch were done by lime. Apart from the place of other house-hold activities, these floors were accomodated with ovens for individual / community cooking. Adjoining environment had supplied enough fuel (branches of trees) for cooking to every individual. Sometimes cut-bones, used as tools were also noticed in these ovens. The process may hardened the cut-bones to serve the purpose of hunting and other activities.

Their efforts also point to the civic senses, as evidenced by the occurrence of garbage pit during the course of re-excavation at Pandurajar Dhibi in 1985.

Thus the structural activities in Eastern India throws enough light on the reconstruction of history during BRW phase.

Notes and References

1. H. N. Singh : History and Archaeology of Black and Red ware, Page : 72, Delhi, 1982.
2. Ibid : Page - 158.
3. Indian Archaeology 1961- 62, A Review. Page : 61.
4. Ibid : Page - 61.
5. Indian Archaeology 1972 - 73, A Review. Page : 8.
6. Indian Archaeology 1970 - 71, A Review. Page : 7.
7. Indian Archaeology 1974 - 75, A Review. Page : 51.
8. Ibid : Page - 77.
9. Indian Archaeology 1983 - 84, A Review. Page : 92 - 93.
10. Indian Archaeology 1986 - 87, A Review. Page : 96.
11. Ibid : Page - 95.
12. Ibid : Page - 94.
13. Exploring Bengal's Past : Edited by P. C. Dasgupta, Page : 22, 1966.
14. Ibid : Page - 23.
15. Shyam Chand Mukherji, Deputy Director of Archaeology, Government of West Bengal : Unpublished Official Report on the Excavation at Pandurajar Dhibi, Burdwan, dated : 8. 8. 1985.

6

MATERIAL ANALYSIS CERAMIC INDUSTRY

The present analysis of ceramic industry of Pandurajar Dhibi is based on excavated materials now housed in the State Archaeological Museum, West Bengal at Behala, Kolkata-700034 under the Directorate of Archaeology and Museum. The major focus of this analysis is related to pottery types, their tentative functional aspects and the frequency of different types, recorded according to their periodisation. We have tried to demonstrate different types of pottery and their relevance in the context of daily use including function besides the continuity of pottery types and change of the same in the successive period on the basis of the analytical frame work. It may also reflect the pottery using culture of the early village farmers as a whole and Pandurajar Dhibi in particular. The other aspects of ceramic tradition like the preparation of clay, the texture of pottery, the fabrication including firing and application of slip are also very important part of our discussion. But due to various limitation, sometimes we failed to demostrate different aspect in a very particular way. Though in some cases we have studied the material as maximum as possible.

The first stage of pottery manufacturing by the early village farmers of Pandurajar Dhibi suggest an utilisation of ordinary clay deposits occuring near Damodar river. These clay contained organic matters and iron compound, including a very small proportion of magnetic oxide. The former became black when heated and only burnt away if the temperature and air supply are sufficient, while the latter, except the magnetic oxide, the clay become converted into red oxide. Regarding the technique, archaeologists have generally believed in what has been described as the "Inverted Firing Technique" where the pots are placed in an inverted position in the kiln, subjecting the exterior to oxidising conditions and the interior to reducing condition. Saw-dust or some vegetable matter might have been filled in the pot while firing under reducing condition. As a result, the interior turns black and the exterior dull red to buff in colour.

The clay used to give a fine paste and sand, quartz, husk or other tempering material is very sparingly used. There can be only two ways in which such pottery could have been made namely

By the simultenous productionn of the red of the body (apart from any wash of red ochre) and the black of the interior and the rim.

By producing the same, wholly red first and then by a secondary operation of blackening the interior of the rim. The red chrome appeared in few instances, was an extremely thin-applied coating.

An analysis of the painted BRW from Pandurajar Dhibi has revealed that both the surfaces were subjected to paintings. Pigments were quarried from river beds or nearby sources. These materials for preparation of pigments were probably crushed with hammer and mixed with juice of water and various vegetable ingredients. In all most all the cases white pigment applied over black and red surfaces while black and cream chrome with subdued tone occurred on lustrous red surface. The analysis and classification also suggest the existence of 14-individual types with 53-sub types. The geometric designs include different varieties of triangles, solid bands, chevron etc. The red ware was probably the most popular subject to be painted with various designs to the early village farming people of Pandurajar Dhibi. The black chorme was the most popular subject as well as seems to have a special appeal to the contemporary people.

Pottery Analysis : BLACK AND RED WARE (here after B. R. W.) Sheet Number 1, 2, 3 & 4 contained the Bar-diagram and Pie-chart of BRW variety such as Bowl (Patra), Cooking vessel (Handi), Vessel (Kalas). Goblet (Khupo), Funnel (Kupi), Channel spouted Bowl.

Sheet Number : 1 (here after S. N. 1)

S.N. 1 represent a pottery type, termed as Bowl (Patra) for eating, drinking and storage of food grains. A total of 100 - specimens have been recorded to classify at least 9 - varieties. These specimens occupied 36.63 % of total B.R.W. samples, excavated from the different layers of Pandurajar Dhibi. The periodisation and the frequency in terms of percentage and number, envisages the following information.

Type number V have been occurred in all the four periods within a time bracket ranging from C. 1600 B.C. - C.300 B.C. The total samples in this category are six and thus occupied 2.19 % of the total collection of 273 specimens. Another type, numbering XXIV appeared from C. 1200 B.C, and continued upto C. 300 B.C. with 35 samples and occupied 12.82 % of the total collection. Next to this, a type with 23 samples seems to appear in the scene from C.600 B.C. to C.300 B.C. with a percentage of 8.42 %

among the total specimens. The other types are six in number with a total of 36 samples. Among these types, a total of 18 samples included in the type number VIII (C.600 B.C. to 200 A.D.) while the other types are II, IX, XIX, XXII (C.900 B.C. to 300 B.C.). Our analysis further shows the importance of item number 1, for eating, drinking and storage in comparasion to other items.

Sheet Number : 2 S.N. 2 envisages ten varieties of cooking vessel (Handi). There are altogether 108 samples in these ten varieties suggesting the occurrence of 39.56 % in 273 specimens. The periodisation and frequency in terms of percentage and number delineates the following information.

Type number XXIII with 92 samples of excavated BRW from Pandurajar Dhibi have been noticed in all the four periods, having a time bracket ranging from C. 1600 B.C. to C. 300 B.C. The remaining nine types with 18 samples finds their place from C. 1200 B.C. to 200 A.D. (5 samples), C 900 B.C. to C 600 B.C. (2 samples), and from C. 600 B.C. to C 300 B.C. (11 samples). Our analysis further demonstrate the popularity of type number XXIII due to it's maximum occurrence.

Sheet Number : 3 S.N. 3 delineates no less than four types of B.R.W. with a sub-type in one case. The main types are vessel (kalasa), Goblet (khupo), Funnel (kupi) and Channel spouted bowl. Among these four types, channel spouted bowl with 35-samples occupied 12.82 % and vessel (kalasa) with 16-samples ensure 9.89 % among 273 specimens. The other two types included goblet and funnel represent 0.36 % and 0.73 % respectively may suggest their occassional use. Our analysis also highlighted the maximum use of cooking vessels (39.56 %). Next to cooking vessel, there are two major types of bowls of which one is channel spouted bowl and the other is general. The former type of bowl had a certain use, probably related with offering as well as drinking.

The samples of goblet (0.36 %) and funnel (0.73 %) suggest their limited use in the society. Apart from these four types, the last significant items are vessel (kalasa : 9.89 %) and bowl (Patra : 36.63 % of S.N. 4).

Pottery Analysis : BLACK WARE (here after B. W.)

Sheet Number 5, 6, 7, 8 & 9 contained the Bar-diagram and Pie-chart of B.W. variety such as Dish (Patra), Cooking vessel (handi), Channel spouted Bowl

(Nala-sambalita patra), Dish-on-stand (sasthambha thali), Fry Pan (kada), Vessel (kalas).

Pandurajar Dhibi has yielded B. W. beside B.R.W. and R.W. in ten different types. Both the interior and exterior surfaces of total 133 - specimens were coated with black slip. One of the interesting feature of this kind of pot-sherds is the absence of painting and introduction of incision, particularly the faunal depiction. The similarity in the shape of B.R.W. and B.W. also suggest that they full-filled the requirements of same group of peoples. Some manufacturing diversity may be the reason of the difference in colour. Sometimes the pieces of discarded BRW have been coated with black-slip to designate it as Black ware. Though BRW has yielded a good number of channel spouted bowl, they are completely different from that of BW. The shape, size, broadness of channel and above all the dignity and quality of the former variety surpasses to a great extent in comparison with the channel spouted bowl of BW variety. The latter envisages a complete degeneration regarding it's shape and other quality with that of the former.

Our analysis clearly suggest the preponderance of only three types among the proposed ten varieties, Of these items, general bowl 32.28 %, Dish : 26.29 %, and channel spouted bowl : 21.05% have the major share in the total 133 specimens. The other important items are Cooking vessel (Handi), Flower vase (phuldani), Dish-on-stand (Swasthamba thali), Fry-pan (Kada), Vessel (Kalasa), Basin (gamla), and Trough (Jabna-bhanda).

The maximum occurrence of BW started from period II and reached it's peak during period III and IV. Out of 133 specimens, 83-samples have been occurred during these periods. Occurrence of Basin (gamla), and Trough (jabna-bhanda) clearly suggest some sort of cattle breeding during the later phase of the early village farming community at Pandurajar Dhibi.

Pottery Analysis : RED WARE (here after R. W.)

Sheet Number 10, and 11 contained the Bar-diagram and Pie-chart of R.W. variety such as Cooking vessel (Handi), Bowl (patra), Vessel (kalasa). Channel spouted Bowl (Nala-sambalita patra),

Excavated RW assemblage of Pandurajar Dhibi consisted of 38 specimens. It appeared in the scene from period II and continued upto period IV i.e. a time bracket ranging from C. 1200 BC to C. 300 BC. All the 38 specimens of RW are classified into 9-types. The early inhabitants of Pandurajar Dhibi used frequently some cooking vessel (Handi), Bowl (Patra), and Basin (Gamla) of red ware as their kitchen utencil beside BRW and BW. Among these three types, cooking vessel of red ware occurred in maximum number. The other noteworthy types are bowl, basin, vessel, dish, funnel shaped pot, juice or wine container, ghata and channel spouted bowl. The channel spouted bowl of BW appeared in the scene from 900 BC and continued upto 600 BC while the same type of bowl in RW appeared from 600 BC and continued upto 300 BC. The sudden disappearance of channel spouted bowl in BW was supplanted by RW variety probably indicate some changes in contemporary society. Our analysis further delineates the emergence of a particular type of pottery, appeared and disappeared from a particular period, giving way to new types with multipurpose use.

A Suggested Inventory of SHAPES, SIZES, FUNCTIONAL aspects of major pottery types Pandurajar Dhibi, Burdwan, West Bengal BLACK AND RED WARE

Type - I

This type is represented by 23-specimens, has different shapes, ranging from large to tiny. The featureless internally curved rim, finally shaped a bowl with rounded base. The texture varies and the profile indicates the preparation of well lavigated clay. There are few specimens with strokes of white painting on external and internal surface. The shape and the type commonly resemble with modern day pottery, oftenly used for frying rice.

Type - II

This type is represented by 8-specimens, has different shapes, ranging from large to tiny. The bowl with straight / vertical body including rim specially made for big sized container with rounded flat base. The overall shape could be easily compared with that of modern days utensil known as JAMBATI.

Type - III

This is represented by 7-specimens. The vessel having vertical / straight body, curved slightly at the rim. The irregular surface with medium thickness indicate the use of wheel and batting during the course of preparation. Our general reading about the functional aspect of such vessel suggest its use as a container of dry substance of food grains.

Type - IV

This type is represented by 16-specimens. The functional aspect, as indicated by it's incurved mouth suggest it's use as a hoarding container for the preservation of seeds. One could cover the incurved rim / mouth with a lid to get the effect of an air-tight condition. Even today, it is customery to use such type of pottery with the help of permanent cover made of the mixture of cow-dung, earth and straw. The molasses were kept openly in such type of pottery for a long period after covering the mouth with the application of same method.

Type - V

This type is represented by 6-specimens. Both large and tiny shaped pot of this variety suggest different types of functional aspect. The smaller one in our collection might have been used as crusable for black smith while the larger one may serve as container for the preparation of pigments for painting, keeping rice or offering oblation. We have at least two pieces of such type containing painting.

Type - VI

This type is represented by 6-specimens. It is one of the sophisticated rare variety of carinated vessel probably used during special occassion or rather to say manufactured for ceremonial purpose. The well curved rim gradually goes down towards oblique wall of the vessel finally with flattish base. The frequency of size and capacity to contain, reflect that the type probably used by elite class, never used as a heavy duty pottery.

Type - VII

This type is represented by 4-specimens. This typical type of basin having out turned feature less rim with thick vertical body and probably a round base. It may be used as a measuring unit for storing grains.

Type - VIII

This type is represented by 18-specimens. It has festureless incurved rim, possibly used as a container ofmilk product. In rural Bengal, the pottery termed as Khara has very close affinity with the said type. The size vary from large to small where as the rounded base possibly made with the horizontal plan.

Type IX

This type is represented by 5-specimens. This is a bowl with flaring mouth. The featureless externally grooved rim with sharp incurved body possibly had a rounded base. This type of large to medium sized pot probably used for frying rice and known as KHULI to the modern floks.

Type X

This type is represented by only two specimens. This is a carinated bowl having flaring mouth with thick rim. It has obliquely curved neck with convex shoulder. The texture, profile, fineness and rarity of this type indicate it's occasional use, probably for carrying sweets and milk product including sugarcane juice.

Type - XI

This type is represented by a single specimen. The sagar based carinated bowl or Handi had a flaring rim with the small curved neck. Regarding the utiliterian aspect of this specimen, we suggest it's use for the preparation of milk product.

Type XII

This type is also represented by a single specimen. It is a medium sized thick carinated vessel / handi. The splayed out rim along with oblique shoulder display the multipurpose utility of the same.

Type XIII

This type is represented by a single specimen. The slightly curved rim with thick convex shoulder gradually formed the straight profile and probably with black base, resembles with modern jambati of village folk.

Type XIV

This type is represented by a single specimen. It has thick flaring rim with carinated neck. The slighly elongated neck with thick round externally grooved shoulder indicated it's use as a flower vase in the context of present day. The interior black surface bear over the flaring rim and a row of parallel incised band occurred horizontally beside a row of oblique bands with dots above. The convex exterior, red surface near the rim also bear horizontal curving.

Type XV

This type is represented by a single specimen. The flaring mouth and concave short neck of this tiny pot is essential and purposefully prepared. It's oblique shoulder gradually tapers from the mid ridge at the junction between shoulder and body. The functional aspect may be related with the container for the storing of fruit juice or wine.

Type XVI

This type is represented by two specimens. It is a carinated handi with externally splayed out thick rim. The globular body has an even thickness, probably storing temperature.

Type XVII

This type is represented by two specimens. This funnel shaped pottery envisages flaring mouth with concave and elongated neck possibly connected with it's globular body. It is probably a typical container used as scientific instrument like modern days laboratory funnel. However, the utility of such pottery for the preparation of medicinal herbal lequid / paste may not be ruled out.

Type XVIII

This type is also represented by a couple of specimens. It is a small and painted handi with carination at the neck having oblique shoulder. This particular feature has rendered it a round base. The thick external rim having paintings on the inner side of the mouth and size suggest it's probable use as a ritualistic container.

Type XIX

This type is represented by three specimens. It is a small carinated bowl with splayed out featureless rim had thick shoulder with rounded body and used as cooking vessel, has been occurred in different BRW sites of West Bengal such as Bharatpur, Pakhanna, Mangalkot etc. Such occurrence also shows it's day to day utility in the house, of contemporary village farmer.

Type XX

This type is represented by a single specimen. The flaring mouth of the pot with internally levelled rim delineates carinated and slightly curved neck along with convex shoulder formed a round vessel with flat base. The shape and size resembles with present day Jambati.

Type XXI

This type is represented by a single specimen. The out turned rim relatively thin towards the edge, projected the huge body with short neck, curved uniquely. The size and shape of the vessel suggest it's occassional use for the preparation of special dish which required temperature both from upper and lower part.

Type XXIII

This type is represented by a single specimen. This special type of table ware having straight body with slanting base and the rim with medium thickness, splayed out horizontally from the neck. The shape and total craftsmanship comparable with modern Dekchi, might have been used in special occassion. The janapada site including Taxila has revealed the existence of such type of pottery.

Type XXIII

This type is represented by 90 specimens. This is a carinated handi / cooking vessel, found in different sizes. It has out turned but internally levelled rim with carinated neck and rounded profile. As the site has yielded this type of cooking vessel / handi in numerous sizes, a close observation resulted it's utility, particularly for the preparation of boiled rice. Some large sized pottery in the present collection throw enough light about the rate of consumption including its utility towards heavy duty. Therefore, we may assume that this type of pottery served small family as well as bigger one.

On the other hand, we may put forward our next suggestion regarding the way of consumption of various types of such vessels.

Our collection helps us to formulate the functional use as that the different sizes of such vessels, might have arranged vertically by following bigger to smaller container, placed on the oven for boiling. The other vessels arranged vertically by following bigger to smaller container placed one after another. In this process, it is obvious that the boiling temperature of the lower vessel will generate requisite temperature for boiling food grains of the remaining vessels. The process might have useful for reduction of fuel consumption as well as period of preparation. It is worth mentioning that such type of practice is in vogue at temple complex of Jagannath at Puri even today.

Type XXIV

This type is represented by 35 specimens. It is designated as the Channel spouted bowl with traces of paintings in translucent white chrome on the interior black surface. The type made it's first a appearance in period II and continued upto period IV having a time bracket ranging from C 1200 BC to C 300 BC. The typical Channel spouted bowl of BRW of all periods bear a layer of red slip on the exterior surface with an almost uniform thickness of 0.5 cms and dia 10.5 cms.

The Channel spouted bowl of Pandurajar Dhibi occupy an important place among the other pottery types of the site. They were found from Crete, Anatolia and Iran in the abroad and Ahar Navdatoli, Eran, Sonpur and some other sites in South India and Eastern India. The Iranian origin of the Channel spouted bowls has not been favoured by some scholars, who insisted to Crete, Anatolia and China.

In this context the Sauce boat - type handled bowls or cups (with a ring at the base and a cut spout fitted to the mouth) found in the middle level at Larna, C.2000 BC. in Crete and other places in mainland Greece may be profitably compared with similar bowls from Pandurajar Dhibi.

In India, this type of bowls must have originated some where in Central India and Ganga Yamuna doab and that too, possibly during post Harappan Chalcolithic times. At Pandurajar Dhibi, a good number of such bowls (one intact) in BRW have been found from period II and III. Such bowls in black slipped ware were also found from period IV.

Thus it appears that this particular ceramic industry was popular with the people of the Ajay valley and it's neighbourhood in Bengal and Bihar.

Utilization of this type of bowls is still a mystery to us but on the basis of Larna Sauce boat and jip like shape of the Channel spouts, it may be observed that they were used for drinking wine or water and not perhaps for ritualistic (cf. Hindu Brahmanical Kosa- kusi) purpose. The Channel spouted bowls or basins were perhaps known to the Rgveda Aryans for drinking Soma-juice.

Verses IX.1.2. & IX. 75.3. of the Rgveda : "Pavamana soma - Suktavisvacarsanirabhi Yonimahatyam Druna Sadasthamasadat II &........ Kosa A hiranyaye I" may refer to a golden channel spout. Eastern India or Gauda Desa has been regarded by Panini (C.5th Cent. BC.) as a great producer of molasses and honey of various kinds, and it is known that fermented molasses (very lequid) was used as a kind of wine.Hence the efficacy of Channel spouted bowls in Eastern India, cannot be ruled out.Mukherje : 1967.

Red Ware

Type I.

This type of carinated bowl / handi is represented by five specimens. The texture, thickness, surface treatment and the application of slip altogether exhibit a well represented type corresponding with late BRW phase at the site. The sharp out turned curved neck and some how slanting body obliquely incurved to form a very determinestic shape of a bowl / handi. It's central axis possibly tubular in shape representing the manufacturing of fast moving wheel. Regarding the utility of such pottery, we may assume that it might have been used for multipurpose cooking as well as storing milk product.

Type II

This type of high-necked vessel is represented by four specimens. The balance between the upper part and the lower one is divided by a central axis. The out turned sort rim suggest the provision for carrying as well as other utility of the vessel. The general shape of such vessel found as boiling utensil including the preparation of rice. Though the type is represented by four specimens, the vessel seems to be very popular in day to day purpose.

Type III

This type which is small in shape is represented by three specimens. The thick headed, out turned rim of the extant portion suggest a pot with narrow neck. The lower part of the body might be globular in shape, probably used for carrying water.

Type IV

This symmetrical type of basin is represented by three specimens. The flaring mouth, out turned rim and incurved body including its central axis exhibit the absorbing capacity of heat. Though designed with the depiction of some geometric motifs, usually such type of pottery has the utility for the preparation of frying cereals, presently known as Khapuri in rural areas.

Type V

This type of bowl is represented by two specimens. The blunted featureless rim with curved body gradually meet the central base in such a manner which in turn could be used for storage or cooking purpose. It is generally found in stone and known as Khara, to offer holy water of Ganges or milk product. So the possibility of it's use for religious purpose may not be turn down.

Type VI

This type of heavy duty carinated vessel is represented by two specimens. The incurved body reached it's central axis to form a round base.

Type VII

This type of bowl is represented by two specimens. According to available part of the pot and it's subsequent reconstruction, it may be a correct speculation that the bowl might have been used for the preparation of pigment by the contemporary potters of Pandurajar Dhibi.

Type VIII

This type is represented by two specimens. The existing part of this type indicate it's use as a vessel for drinking water. The splayed out rim with thick body beside the preparation of neck altogether suggest it's utility for storing lequid, obviously water.

Type IX

The extant part of this type of bowl is represented by two specimens. The featureless blunted rim, sharply incurved body, probably indicate it's use as a container for warming prepared food.

Type X

This type of handi, specially made for the preparation of sweet rice-porridge is represented by two specimens. The out turned rim, obliquely curved body gradually goes down towards a flat base at it's central axis. The texture with application of other technicalities represent the amount of manufacturing.

We may also assume that the type might have used for both secular and religious purpose.

Type XI

This type of bowl is represented by a single specimen. The featureless internally curved rim with round base and concave body may correspond with present day Khola / Hola. The type also finds it's place in BRW variety as well as late phase of BRW.

Type XII

This type of large vessel is represented by a single specimen. The out turned rim, incurved body and presence in other variety of pottery indicate its use for the purpose of heavy duty.

Type XIII

This type is represented by a single specimen. The funnel shaped pottery is also available in other variety. The flaring mouth with steady rim, bluntly ended on top is the indicator of it's special use already discussed earlier. But the difference existed here about the length of the mouth and absence of other portion of the funnel shaped vessel. Therefore it is very difficult to speculate it's actual functional aspect.

Type XIV

This type is represented by a single specimen envisaging a bowl with featureless blunt rim. The incurved body generally form a round dish shape resemble with present day container of curds.

Type XV

This type of medium sized vessel is represented by a single specimen. It may be designated also as a bowl, with lotus petalled out turned rim, blunted towards the top. The body which is coming down sharply from the neck of the vessel gives a particular shape contrast with flaring mouth. The functional aspect may be assumed after comparing with it's present counterpart. The container might have been used for mixing repeatedly the milk or juice of medicinal herbs.

Type XVI

This type of incurved bowl is represented by a single specimen. It is also available in other variety. The blunted rim with weavy neck continued towards incurved body gradually form a tapering base.

Type XVII

This is a typical vessel(Kalasa) with splayed out rim. It is represented by a single specimen. The oblique neck, extended with curved body forming the flat based container / vessel. The rim and thin section indicate it's religious or household utility.

Type XVIII

This type is represented by two specimens. The extant part envisages only the rear half of the channel spouted bowl of red ware variety. It also delineates qualitative deterioration in comparison with earlier variety.

Black Ware

Type I

This type is represented by 26 specimens. It is a medium sized plate with curved blunt rim. The gently curved slanting body has rendered a shallow interior. An uniform thickness has been maintained throughout the body of the plate.

Type II

This type is represented by 9 specimens. It is also occurred in the BRW assemblage. Though the inner part is concave, the blunted rim with slightly twisted at the upper, exhibit the difference and quality. The thickness of the profile as well as the texture is medium in shape. The slightly tapering upper part probably help to carry it by fingers.

Type III

This type is represented by 4 specimens. It is a plate type pot demonstrating an artistic execution. It's small twised rim help to originate it's curved body gently covered it's base with flattish shape. It's texture is also medium in shape possibly indicating one of the precious item of this category of ceramic.

Type IV

This type of plate is represented by 5 specimens and prepared for different purpose as suggested by the rim portion. It is bold enough and slightly out turned resulting a minimum twist to form the neck as well as the rest of the body. This kind of pot with shallow interior may also indicate the choice of the contemporary buyer who prefer to maintain more sophisticated life.

Type V

This type is represented by 9 specimens. It is a typical bowl, generally associated with waste material of modern farming community, locally known as " Chuto handi ". It is a typical type of pottery to carry light substance including delicious food. The blunt top with sharp and curved rim continued up to base indicating the use of foot rest as a stand of such type of bowl.

Type VI

This type is represented by 5 specimens. It is also a carinated bowl, generally present in BRW assemblage. The out turned rim with curved / slanting neck forms the part of bowl with curved body. It's medium texture and concave interior display its functional aspect during the course of cooking activity.

Type VIII

This type is represented by 4 specimens. It is a carinated bowl with thick wall and deep rim. The sharp and extended rim, out turned sharply towards curved body with an essential feature of tapering. The specimen might have been used as a container of prepared food rather than used during the course of cooking.

Type VIII

This type is represented by 3 specimens only. It is well finished curved bowl with blunt rim. The twisted rim gradually going down to it's curved body and finally rest on a flattish base. Such type of bowl was also available in Black and Red ware assemblage.

Type IX

This type is represented by 3 specimens. It is a large bowl with obliquely turned body. This type of sharp twisted rim is also noticed in BRW - variety. The carrying capacity as exposed by the thick section exhibit it's utility for heavy duty purpose during the course of cooking food.

Type X

This type is represented by 3 specimens. It is a small sized carinated handi, very popular in village house hold for the preparation of milk product. The splayed out rim, curved small neck and gradually convexed body altogether help to form an idea about the shape of the vessel. The fine texture and the application of slip beside firing are the other components, responsible for it's steadiness.

Type XI

This type is represented by 2 specimens. It is also a carinated handi with flaring mouth. The vertical neck and the length of the out - turned rim, thickness of the section as well as existing shape denote it's multipurpose utility.

Type XII

This type is represented by 2 specimens. It is a fascinating bowl with twisted rim, gradually reached at it's blunt head. The middle axis of the pottery sharply slanting towards a flat base. The shallow space with medium texture also indicate it's fineness.

Type XIII

This type is represented by 2 specimens. This sort of big vessel occurred in large quantity in BRW asemblage. The out turned rim curved to meet it's vertical wall, could be designed as modern days elongated Dekchi. The pottery with medium texture bear some painting. The depth of the inner space also suggest it's use as a heavy duty container. Such type of pottery generally used for storing grains, preparation of food in large scale or carrying prepared food.

Type XIV

This type is represented by 2 specimens. It is a shallow dish or plate. The incurved twisted rim gradually extended towards a flat horizontal base. Regarding the functional aspect of the type it seems that the pot may serve as a container of special gift or prestigious item for any member of the society. It could be a prototype of porcelain dish or plate, found in the assemblage of Chaldean pottery in South Indian ceramic industry. (Dasgupta : 1964).

Type XV

This type is represented by two specimens. It is a common pottery type present in the BRW assemblage. The type could be designated as the prototype of modern days measuring unit of grains known as Dhama. The presence of painting at the central part, thickness of the wall and other aspect suggest it's application as a measuring unit.

Type XVI

This type is represented by 2 specimens. It is a bowl with conical base with a very small twisted rim. The slanting body reach at the base while the flaring mouth envisages the functional aspect as an offering bowl.

Type XVII

This type is represented by 2 specimens. It is a typical bowl, very much occurred in BRW assemblage and prepared with a careful mind for the determination of balance between the rim part and the body of the pottery. Though aesthetically, the bowl delineates some sophisticated feature, yet it is very difficult to believe it's association with daily use. The out turned rim, slightly curved neck and slanting body extended up to base.

Type XVIII

This type is represented by 2 specimens. It is also a bowl with carinated rim, looks like a beak, internally curved at the neck.

Thus, the shape envisages an extended concave body, curved externally gradually ended towards a round base.

Type XIX

This type is represented by 2 specimens. It is a carinated handi (cooking vessel). The blunt rim, grooved externally while the entire body demonstrate a vessel having an angular shape & flat base. The shape resembled with present day metal cooking vessel.

Type XX

This type is represented by a single specimen. The variety also occurred in BRW assemblage. The type demonstrating a flaring mouth, sharply bent towards neck and turned vertically to render a funnel shape with globular body. Regarding the functional aspect, we may assume that it is related either with the container of medicinal components or a kind of jug, found in modern days.

Type XXI.

This type is represented by a single specimen. It is relatively a large vessel, looked like a dekchi, though not carinated. The blunt rim slighly curved at the neck and attached with straight vertical body ended into flat base. The preparation of rim and the thickness of the section envisages a consistency in terms of texture.

Type XXII

This type is represented by a single specimen. It is a typical bowl with blunt rim twisted slightly at it's interior. The well maintained curved body gradually forming it's base.

Type XXIII

This type is represented by a single specimen. It is a carinated bowl, tiny and conical in shape with a thick section. The central axis and the balance of forming the body demonstrate the articulation of potter's control over the wheel.

Type XXIV

This type is represented by a single specimen. It is a shallow bowl, apparently a basin shape having out turned carinated rim. The curved slanting body extended to it's flat base while the inner space indicate it's utility for a special type of bowl / basin alternatively used serving any item. The pot may equally served the purpose of a plate.

Type XXV

This type is represented by a single specimen. It is an unique type of tiny bowl, could be termed as Kopta to the present folks of West Bengal. The finished part of the body and the painting with overall shape indicate it's speciality towards serving precious item.

Type XXVI

This type is represented by a single specimen. It is a curved bowl with internally twisted rim and blunted head. The gently curved body helps to form a round base. The inner space might have suggested a deep room for storing food or other items. The aesthetic sense of the upper part of the existing pottery suggest makers control on the wheel.

Type XXVII

This type is represented by a single specimen. It is a tiny pot. The extant portion exhibit a blunt in, slightly curved out wardly at the top. The externally curved high necked rim, bented gradually towards the interior space in the shape of globular formation. Though the central axis and the curving texture of the pottery section delineates a delicate handling of wheel as well as the determinestic preparation of such type of pottery, found in different early historic site including Rajghat, Taxila etc. The functional aspect may suggest it's use as a container of fruit juice or wine.

Type XXVIII

This type is represented by 7 specimens and designated as Channel spouted bowl of inferior quality comparing with channel spouted bowl of BRW variety. The size and breadth of the channel of the BR - variety became small and short in comparison with BRW specimens.

Type XXIX

This type is represented by two specimens. The extent part envisages a shallow dish gradually slanting towards an elongated stand with flat circular base.

7

COMPERATIVE STUDY

Black and Red ware (Here after BRW), subsequently discovered in different parts of our country, with different chronological contexts, proposed the begining of settlement history with a rural character. The structural remains found in association with the BRW throughout India, envisages a rural character, though there are few sites having sophestication of living style, could be assumed as semi - urban. The quantitative analysis of BRW sites, acquainted us with the divergencies which could be noticed in the different aspects of material culture.[1.]

In this chaper, a thorough discussion on material remains of BRW period put forward to highlight a scope ofcomparison with inter sites characteristics. Although it would be a suggestive method to incorporate the entire available data in Indian context, but our scope here is restricted with the data base from Eastern India. The following calibrated C-14 dates from Eastern India clearly suggest the existence of full fledged sedantism along the middle and lower ganga valley by about 2000 B.C., if not earlier.[2.]

1)	Sonpur	-	Circa. 800 B.C.	-	425 B.C.[3.]
2)	Chirand	-	Circa. 2195 B.C.	-	1750 B.C.[4.]
3)	Bharatpur	-	Circa.1770 B.C.	-	1410 B.C.[5.]
4)	Bahiri	-	Circa. 900 B.C.	-	660 B.C.[6.]
5)	Arra	-	Circa.1110 B.C.	-	810 B.C.[7.]
6)	Hatikhera	-	Circa. 900 B.C.[8.]		
7)	Mahishdal	-	Circa.1690 B.C.	-	1405 B.C.[9.]
8)	Mangalkot	-	Circa.1000 B.C. [10.]		
9)	Pakhana	-	Circa.1500 B.C. [11.]		
10)	Pandurajar Dhibi	-	Circa.1600 B.C.	-	300 B.C. [12.]

The above summary of chronological ranges available through C-14 dates clearly demonstrate that, by about 2000 B.C. the full fledged sedantism existed in Eastern India particularly along the Ganga valley (middle and lower). The region received a major exploitation of land during this time by the early settlers. In the subsequent period these early settlers arrived in South Bihar plain resulting the emergence of BRW sites like UREN, NONAGARH, ABHAYPUR, KAZRA, SUDAMDIH, KHERIPAHAR, CHAMPA, JHIM-JHIMAIYA KALISTHAN, etc. [13.] In this context, it is worth mentioning that the spread of BRW culture in the lower Gangetic plain, particularly the Ajay, Damodar, Dwarakeswar valley received the expansion of BRW people from South Bihar plain by following the route along the river valley. Our comperative data presented here certainly had a number of limitation, but the C - 14 dates available from this region definitely suggest the colonisation of early farming community in Bharatpur, Pandurajar Dhibi, Mahishdal, Pakhanna and other sites around 1600 B.C., if not earlier.

While discussing the technical process of pottery manufacturing developed by the BRW people, we may present the problem in the following way. The large scale production of BRW require a sizeable infrustructure and evolved technology including the standardization of the lavigation of clay, use of different types of wheel, the different stages of preparation of clay and above all the most significant is the firing technique. It is well known that since the theorization of Sir Mortimer Wheeler, the scholarly world extended their view point about the technical aspect of BRW and the context of firing always received attention by the scholars.

Beside diverse cultural feature, this ware also carries varied contextual personality. The Eastern Indian BRW culture is completely different from that of rest of India. Even we noticed a blatant diversity in the chronological background as stated earlier.

This ware is a product of inverted firing technique where the pots are placed in an inverted position in the kiln, subjecting the exterior to oxidising condition and the interior to reducing condition. Saw dust or some vegetable matters might have been filled in the pot while firing under reducing conditions. As a result, the interior turns black and the exterior dull red to buff in colour.[14.]

The technical personality of this ware seems to be very much diverse in nature as evidenced by three different manufacturing techniques such as :

1) Single firing technique.
2) Double firing techniques, where the pot is fired red first.
3) Double firing techniques, where the pot is fired black first.

Here we have limited scope to discuss elaborately about more aspects of firing techniques. The brief discussion here may help us to know the gravity of firing process and its close association with large scale production which play an important role in the household economy of village farming community in Eastern India, particularly West Bengal.[15.]

Regarding the structural evidence as gathered from the major sites of India, it has been noticed that Lothal witnessed the construction of brick structure while Ahar revealed the structures of undressed blocks of Schiest and mud. In this context for our broad understanding about the general character of BRW settlement in different landscape of India in every possibility, Aharian housing pattern deserves our special attention. So we may have a look about the specific information on structural evidence reported from Ahar.[16.]

The excavator of Ahar clearly demonstrated the different subclassification of habitional pattern by following a consistent character of change, exhibit the requirement of BRW people through contrast situation. The more information about the successive changing pattern of habitational layer unfolded during excavation throws enough light about the similarities or contrast between Ahar and Pandurajar Dhibi. The similarities has been observed in the formative settlement pattern of the habitat of both Ahar and Pandurajar Dhibi was an elevated landscape to laid the foundation of their incepient housing complex. The contrastness has been tested when we are dealing the second habitational set up recorded at Ahar given a foundation of rubble stone which is totally absent in the context of Pandurajar Dhibi. The third habitation reported from Ahar was more or less similar with that of Pandurajar Dhibi, i.e. over the burnt reddish debries of the earlier occupational ruins followed up by a later habitation. The pheripheral outline was formed over the debris of earlier refused material.[17.]

The sites including Maner, Chechar, Jhim-Jhimia Kalisthan had witnessed structures of wattle and daub, mud-plastered reed screened / bamboo screen along with mud walls and wooden post. The ancient site of Chirand is very rich in antiquities, but so far as the structural remains are concerned, it is very poor. The houses were made of mud and bamboos as revealed by thick chunks of rammed reddish earth bearing impression of reeds and bamboos on one side. Walls were plastered with mud. The evidence from Sonpur is similar.[18.]

The following paragraph precisely present a brief summary of the excavation at Mangalkot to give a comprehensive picture of relationship between the site itself and other sites of the region including Pandurajar Dhibi.

The first settlers of Mangalkot lived at one place for a few centuries at a stretch. The excavation resulted in the discovery of evidence of three floors superimposed one above the other. On the basis of excavation report, the pattern of flooring exhibit an uniformity as follows.

The first floor which is traceable at a depth of 2-meter and the second floor has been noticed at a depth of 3-meter. The third floor appeared at a depth of 3.90 meter. The floors encountered in different layers were usually dark brown in colour, comprising rammed earth with cowdang, sand, kankara and pottery chips. The foundation of structural remains that has been observed by the excavator in all most all the cases was sand, played an important role in this regard.

The discovery of Post Holes and reed marks in burnt clay beside a number of hearth were traceable in the different floor level. It is interesting to mention in this context that the excavator was able to trace a highly fragmentary skeleton remains of human being in one house. The room which was found in MGK I has a well laid surki rammed brick soling floor attatched with a brick lined drainage system. The BRW habitation component was totally absent in later period.[19.]

The houses / rooms of Pandurajar Dhibi were built of perishable materials like reed as evident from the occurrence of burnt clay with reed marks. The inhabitants of the site made their settlement on made up sandy silt. Burnt clay tiles probably served as the covering material for the roof. The floors were either smooth lime plastered or of beaten pellety laterite. A pier like construction paved with terra cotta nodules washed with lime and showing a ramp or stair-case. Evidence of post-holes has been noticed during the course of excavation in 1985.[20.]

The structures at Mahisdal were almost same as Pandurajar Dhibi. They comprised of simple huts in which plastered reed was used. Beaten earth strengthened with a soling of rammed terracotta was the characteristic feature of the floor.[21]

The occupational level at Dihar reveals mud floor and post holes. The floors were made of beaten earth, rammed with terracotta nodules and washed with lime.[22]

The analysis of metal objects recovered from Pandurajar Dhibi & it's relationship in the other sites gives us a venue to discuss the history of the use of metal in Eastern India in general and Pandurajar Dhibi in particular. The frequency of metal object contained in our chart number 16 - 19 envisages certain theoritical as well as evidential perspective for the better understanding about the use of metal by Early village farming community. Metal objects, particularly copper occured very rare particularly in Bengal and Bihar in association with BRW. Our study emphasises probable source of raw material, techniques employed in extraction of the metal and the quantity of the metal extracted. The analysis also throw some light on the fact that if there was a copper smelting site in Eastern India.

Moreover, effort should also be made on the process employed on the solid extracted metal for the production of useful artifacts.[23]

The excavation at Pandurajar Dhibi revealed the occurrence of metal objects from period II. They include fish hook, nail-parer, Bangle, ring, eye-pencil, Bead, and interestingly enough a spear- head from period II. A copper wire from Bahiri has been dated to 1000 B.C. Copper had a limited use in Baneswardanga. No copper has been recovered from period I of the said site. Period II has yielded a single ring while period III & IV witnessed the occurrence of copper beads, pellets, bangles, ear-rings, and pendant. Copper has been a constant material in Mangalkot. But they are mostly for making personal adornments except a fish-hook.[24]

In eastern India so far few complete study on slag samples has been made for the metal objects of Bahiri, Mangalkot, and Pandurajar Dhibi. De & Chattopadhyay (1989) analysed the iron saucer of Pandurajar Dhibi. The concentration of potassium was more in inclusions that the matrix which indicated that the smelting was carried in charcoal fire.[25]

Amongst the three specimens of Pandurajar Dhibi analysed by De & Chattopadhyay (1989), two belongs to period II and the third one from period III. The specimen from period II indicated that the smelting was carried below 1100° Centigrades. The study has also revealed that iron smelting was carried out by filling the hearth and stacking the primitive furnace with charcoal. After ignition, alternate layer of ore and charcoal were charged. These specimens were generated at the central portion of the hearth below two tuyeres. The specimen from period III was generated from mixed charge probably using magnetic ore and only one tuyers was used in that furnace.[26.]

The microlithic industry of BRW phase in south Bihar plain was very rich and also during excavation, Chirand proved it's rich collection of microliths. The tools are manufactured mainly on Chalcedony. Though microlithic cores and flakes do occur at Sonpur, not a single tool has been reported from there.[26]

The BRW people of Pandurajar Dhibi used microliths since the begining of their settlement. The comperative study of occurrence of microliths in different BRW sites suggest homogeneity.[27] The industry was slightly different at Mahisdal. It comprised of scraper, lunate, and short blade. The microliths from Baneswardanga proved its scarcity in period I. But period II has yielded point, blade, lunate, tranchet of quartz, chert and chalcedony beside a scraper on a semirolled quartz pebble. [28.] The earliest inhabitants of Mangalkot were depended primarily on the tools made of cut bones. The result from Dihar at Bankura envisages the occurrence of microliths in quartzite, collected from the bed of Dwarakeswar, during the course of preparation.[29]

The excavation at Pandurajar Dhibi, resulted in the discovery of three types of burials. They are Urn-burial, Extended burial and Fractional burial. It is interesting to note in this connection that these burials had enough affinity with the burial recorded from other sites in West Bengal.[30]

The comperative study dealing with faunal remains in the context of BRW phase in Eastern India, our observation indicate the existence of some inconsistency among the sites. The faunal remains of Chirand included bones of fish, animals, and birds.[31.] Some domesticated varieties were unearthed from the cemetary level of Pandurajar Dhibi in the year 1962. They comprised of pig, humped bull and deer.[32.] No faunal remains have been reported from Mahisdal. Some bone tools have been excavated from Dihar. The bones are yet to be identified. Bones of fish, tortoise, jungle-fowl, fox, deer, and so on have been reported from Mangalkot. The antlers were used for making bone tools. The faunal evidence from Pandurajar Dhibi and allied sites exemplified the ecological balance obtaining in the neighbouring forest of the contemporary time. The delicate equilibrium of the forests, resulting from prey-predator interaction, was produced by the counter balancing presence of predators like jackles, wolves, panthers, fishing cats on the one hand and harbivorous such as deer, omnivorous pigs and grain feeding birds on the other hand. Though they possessed some farm animals of their own, they had to depend on hunting economy for sustainance, as the reverrine deluge very often inundated their limited arable land and decimated the farm animals. The people were initially adopted the hunting economy in period I and the exploitation reached its peak in period II. The farm animals included cattle and buffalo.[33.]

The study has very limited scope to give a comprehensive data related to floral remains of BRW phase. The discovered evidence to this subject constrained us to give an overall idea about the exploitation of floral remains, the process of harvesting of domesticated cereals and other floral components. The scene in eastern India was almost same as in other parts of India. During sub-period I-A of Chirand, the floral remains recovered in association with BRW includes reeds and bamboos.[34.] The BRW phase at Pandurajar Dhibi include reed and rice as floral remains. Lumps of mud plaster belonging to the walls of the houses of period I as well as other periods are reported to bear impressions of reed. Apart from the core sections of certain potsherds, recovered in association with BRW from the levels of period I bear the impression of reed. The impression of paddy husks on the core of the pot sherd recovered from period I were identified as cultivated paddey (oryza sativa L Graminae). The same types of floral evidence were also recorded at Mahisdal.[35]

The early village farming society were acquainted with the manufactureing of terracotta objects from the begining of their settlement. But they are mainly related with cult figurines and ornament, particularly beads of various shapes and sizes, though bangles and ear-rings has been noticed in few major sites. The miscellaneous group include terracotta plumb-bob, lamp, crucible, sling-balls, cakes, toy-cart, potter's dabber, discs and whorls. It will be not out of context to mention on the materials for manufacturing bead. In fact all sorts of materials were used by the maker which includes copper, terracotta, as well as semi-precious stones like carnelian agats, jasper, faience, ivory, lapislazuli, sand-stone and shell during the course of it's preparation.[36]

Beads of terracotta, chalcedony and sand stone has been reported from Chirand and sonpur.[37] They are also discovered from Mahisdal in semi-precious stone and steatite. A collection of 25- beads from the excavation at Baneswardanga envisages, 11 pcs terracotta, 12 pcs semiprecious stones, 1 pc faience and 3 pcs copper.[38] Dihar has yielded a single piece of agate bead from period I while a pair of agate beads from period II. Beads of agate, felsper, jedite and haematite has been recorded from Dihar in association of BRW.[39] Beside copper and terracotta, agate amethyst, carnelian, jasper were employed in making beads at Mangalkot.[40]

The sites of the South Bihar played an important role for negotiation of cultural exchange including pottery manufacturing technology. So this region could be treated as buffar zone, at almost for the contextual association of culture spread during BRW- phase in West Bengal.

Chirand in District Saran is the most important site in South Bihar plain where a substantial quantity of plain and painted BRW has been reported. The main shapes are dish on stand, long necked jars, bowls, lipped bowls, basins, troughs, vases, and lotas. Majority of these types, if not all, are infact unknown in other regions of the country. The tradition of painting also has its own individual line of distinguishing character. In certain cases, the BRW from Chirand carried painting in cream over a red surface, a feature absent in other sites of India. There is no place of painting in the BRW of Sonpur, a site in the same region. Moreover, types like Dish-on- stand footed bowl, spout, jug, lota etc. are absent at Sonpur where as at Chirand, they have found in small number as stated earlier. The differences in Bengal and Bihar or amongst the sites in Bihar itself, should not be a source of confusion as there was no migration of the BRW people, as such, from one region to the other or one place to the other. In case of migration of people, it would be impossible to explain the fundamental differences in the potteries of the two regions. Personal tastes, likings and requirements are responsible for the differences.[41]

Dasgupta was of opinion that the painted BRW of Pandurajar Dhibi vaguely resembles to that from Ahar, Gilund, and Navdatoli. Lal has also pointed out that white painted

BRW is reminiscent of it's counterpart in South-Eastern Rajasthan and Central India. According to the report of excavation at Pandurajar Dhibi, the channel spouted bowl of BRW is comparable with the similar type of bowl, recovered from Navdatoli and the copper bowl from Khurdi in Rajasthan.[42]

The excavation at Kolkhanda mound near village Haraipur has yielded plain and painted BRW beside ten extended burial of Children. Period I of Mahisdal has yielded plain and painted variety of BRW. The main shapes are channel spouted bowl, carinated bowl with splayed out rim and convex sided bowl with sagger base. Both black and white chrome are used in painting. Other associated finds comprised of microliths, a flat copper celt, terracotta, bone tools and beads of semi-precious stones like Pandurajar Dhibi and other early village farming sites of West Bengal. A large quantity of charred rice was also recovered from period I at Mahisdal.

Excavations conducted at Mahisdal, Nanur, Dihar, Tamluk, Mangalkot, Bahiri, Hattigra, Bharatpur, Baneswardanga have largely corroborated with the findings encountered at Pandurajar Dhibi. From the perusal of available C_{14} dates of the BRW sites, it is seen that Bharatpur is the earliest one and dates back to C. 1450 B.C. Next come Mahisdal, Birbhum, C. 1285 B.C., and Pandurajar Dhibi comes third i.e. C.1180 B.C. So BRW phase in the third site began probably around 1200 B.C. and continued upto C. 725 B.C., where as at Mahisdal it had a span of nearly 665 years. The iron bearing phase of Pandurajar Dhibi (Pd : III) is C.705 B.C., where as at Mahisdal, it is 615 B.C. (Pd : II). The C_{14} dates of Bahiri and Hattigra are 1000 B.C. to 900 B.C. A wide conflagration seems to have ended the BRW phase in West Bengal as evidenced by the excavation at Pandurajar Dhibi, Mahisdal, Baneswardanga and Mangalkot.

The most remarkable feature of the BRW in eastern India is the painting which is restricted to the inner surface only, though the same was excavated on both the surfaces in south-eastern Rajasthan. Besides this, instead of ceramic, a large number of arrow head in bone, copper and other materials, and bone tools of various other kinds from Chirand, in south Bihar plain, and Pandurajar Dhibi, Mangalkot etc in West Bengal speaks in favour of hunting as the source of subsistence of these early village farmers, though at later stage, agriculture was also introduced. The occurrence of polished celts in later period at certain sites like Sonpur and Chirand are of a great significant in this context.

Notes & References

1. H. N. Singh : History and Archaeology of Black and Red Ware, Delhi, 1982, Page - : 421 to 425.
2. Ibid - Page : 421 to 425.

3. G. L. Poessehl : Radio Carbon Dates from South Asia, Man and Environment, Volume XII, Pune, Maharashtra, 1988, Page : 195.
4. Ibid - Page : 174.
5. Ibid - Page : 173.
6. Ibid - Page : 186.
7. Ibid - Page : 170.
8. Indian Archaeology 1981 - 85 A Review. Page : 97 and 98.
9. G. L.Poessehl : Radio Carbon dates from South Asia, Man and Environment, Volume : XII, Page : 171.
10. Amita Ray and Samir Mukherjee : Excavation at Mangalkot, Pratna Samiksha,Volume : 1,1991, Page : 121.
11. One the basis of personal communication to Professor Manju Banerjee, Department of Botany, University of Calcutta.
12. Indian Archaeology 1986 - 87 A Review. Page : 95.
13. Chakrabarti et.al. 1995. Preliminary observations on the distribution of archaeological sites in the south-Bihar plain. South Asian Studies, No.-11, Page : 129-147.
14. H. N.Singh : History and Archaeology of Black and Red Ware, Page : 63 and 64, Delhi, 1982.
15. Ibid - Page : 57 to 65.
16. Ibid - Page : 137 to 148.
17. Ibid - Page : 149 to 150.
18. R. K. Chattopadhyay & R. Sanyal - Context and content of Historical Archaeology of South Bihar Pain (Forth-coming).
19. Amita Ray and Samir Mukherjee : Excavation at Mangalkot, Pratna Samiksha, Volume : 1, 1992, Page : 107 to 123.
20. P. C. Dasgupt : The excavation at Pandurajar Dhibi, 1964, Page : 19 - 27.
21. Indian Archaeology 1986 - 1987 A Review. Page : 94 and 95.
22. Anil Chandra Pal : Dihar : A Chalcolithic Site, Pratna Samiksha, Volume -1, Kolkata, 1992, Page - 102.
23. P. K. Chattopadhyay : Principles and modern techniques in the studies of Archaeo-materials in Eastern India, Science in Archaeology and archaeo-materials in Eastern India, Edited by Dr. A. K. Biswas, New Delhi, Page : 315 & 316.
24. Ibid - Page : 319.
25. Ibid - Page : 326.

26. Ibid - Page : 326.
27. Indian Archaeology 1963 - 64 A Review, Page - 59 & 60.
28. S.C. Mukherji : Excavation at Baneswar Danga, District : Bardhaman, Pratna Samiksha, Volume : 2 & 3, 1993 - 94, Page : 80 - 123.
29. D. K. Chakrabarti in Birbhum, Puratattva : An Archaeological Reconnassane : 10, Page 25 - 32.
30. Indian Archaeology 1971 - 72 A Review. Page : 6 and 7.
31. P. C. Dasgupta : The Excavation at Pandurajar Dhibi, 1964, Kolkata, Page : 24.
32. Ibid, Page : 24.
33. Manomoy Ghosh : Animal Remains from Baneswar-danga and it's affinity to other Chalcolithic sites in the District of Bardhaman, Pratnasamiksha, Volume: 2 & 3, 1993-94, Page : 146, 147.
34. H.N. Singh : History and Archaeology of Black and Red Ware, Delhi, 1982, Page : 157, 158.
35. S. C. Mukherji : Chalcolithic Image of West Bengal with special reference to Pandurajar Dhibi, Indian Museum Buletin, 1967, Kolkata, Page : 39 - 49.
36. P. C. Dasgupta : The Excavation at Pandurajar Dhibi, 1964, Kolkata, Page : 28, 29.
37. Indian Archaeology 1971 - 1972 A Review. page : 6 & 7.
38. S. C. Mukherji : Excavation at Baneswardanga, District : Bardhaman, Pratna samiksha, Volume : 2 & 3, Kolkata, 1993 - 94, Page : 108 - 110.
39. Anil Chandra Pal : Dihar : A chalcolithic site, Pratna samiksha, Volume : 1, Kolkata, 1992, Page : 120 - 121.
40. Amita Ray and Samir Mukherjee : Excavation at Mangalkot, Pratna Samiksha, Volume - 1, Kolkata : 1992, Page : 120, 121.
41. H. N. Singh : History and Archaeology of Black and Red Ware, Delhi, 1982, Page :
42. P. C. Dasgupta : The Excavation at Pandurajar Dhibi, 1964, Kolkata, Page : 22 - 24.

8

OTHER OBJECTS RELATED TO SUBSISTANCE / CULTURAL PATTERN. ANALYSIS OF BONE AND ANTLER OBJECTS

Sheet Number 12, 13, 14, and 15 envisages the Bar-diagram and Pie-chart of 92 Bone and Antler objects.

The objects of bone and antler increased in number and variety in the BRW assemblage of Pandurajar Dhibi. The available excavated materials after classification envisages the entire perspective of technological innovation and it's association with bone and antler. Classification of worked bone industry delineates various functional themes although the Zoological study has revealed the nature of consumption of different types of species. Some attempt has been made to identify BRW facies on the basis of pattern variation between assemblages. The tendency of utilisation of bone in different aspect of the life of BRW people convinced us first categorisation of them in a broader perspective. The available typological classification of bone objects represent the various aspects of activity and the nature of consumption of animals during BRW phase at Pandurajar Dhibi. Beside the economy, if any, related to fishing, hunting, scraping, sewing, skin-work, decoration & ornamentation, weaving and other aspects based on bone tools, we have enormous evidence for indicating the ranking of bone tool users including their hierarchy. The highly polished worked bone objects at Pandurajar Dhibi indicate it's major concentration as well as their large scale utilisation including decoration and ornamentation.

The report on the analysis of bone objects carried out by Zoological Survey of India, helped us to know the nature of utilisation of domesticated and wild varieties of animal including acquatic specimens. Interestingly, our stratigraphical evidence including cultural pattern of different phases exhibit the consumption of both wild and domesticated animal bone for the preparation of worked bone. The industry also display a durable character in terms of their strength. The choice of raw material for the manufacturing of bone tool as well as specialisation of working group was also a leading factor in the industrial development of BRW level in general.

The excavation at Pandurajar Dhibi has yielded 92 + bone and antler objects. Sheet number 12 to 15 clearly demonstrate that majority of these bone and antler objects may be classified as hunting tools. Period I has yielded a single piece of bead beside 12 pieces of hunting tool including point, antler, socketed arrowhead and blade. It is interesting to note in this connection that the number of bone objects decreased in period II and III (10 & 7 pieces respectively). The role of substituting bone and antler objects was played neither by metal objects nor stone implements. Period II has witnessed the occrrence of six points and four socketed arrowhead while period III had yielded five socketed arrowhead & two points. Thus our analysis envisages 10.87% and 7.60% of cut bone objects during period II & III. Both manufacturing and use of bone objects increased to a great extent in period IV as evidenced by it's occurrence of 65.23%. The manufacturing of socketed arrow head (25) and Point (12) outnumbered the other varieties like Borer(4), Antler(4), Arrow-head(2), Dagger(2), Chisel(2), Awl(1), Stylus(1), Pin(1), Blow-pipe(1), Nail(1), Scraper(1), Blade(1), Bangle(1), and a single piece of decorated bone piece. Increase of population and probably self-manufacturing process was responsible for this development. Moreover occurrence of flood may reduce their agricultural land and as such they have to depend more on hunting economy beside limited agriculture. The next period has yielded only two points suggesting complete dependance on metal.

The available data from cut bone objects received through excavation at Pandurajar Dhibi and other sites of Eastern India clearly associated with hunting, sewing and weaving activities of the early village farming communities of these area under discussion. Sickle-half and ornamental specimens are the next category of common implements recorded so far in our assemblage. Finally implements associated with skin working, fishing and hair dressing round out the inventory. Implements related to hunting consist of various bone point deserved special mention. Although point have tradiionally been associated with fishing, their presence in the contemporary environmental setting implied that they were more likely used for hunting. Specimens though to have been used for weaving and sewing include awls, borers, slender point for piercing, Sickle half, typically made from split bone were reworked or decorated with a parallel line or net pattern, and even turtle shale are common to other bone artefacts. Hafting recorded from different layers of Pandurajar Dhibi, minutely retouched into the beautiful top. Sickle half were also found from Pandurajar Dhibi, that still contained some other kinds of element. Fishing implements are widely distributed though the same implements of other materials occur in substantial number.

The emergence of an elaborate worked bone industry in association with other varieties of implements may be explained as a result of secure economic condition prevailed among the BRW population of Pandurajar Dhibi and other sites of Eastern India. Moreover, with this socio-economic gain, the BRW phase in and around Pandurajar Dhibi emerged in sharp contrast to the previous microlithic bearing hunting and gathering group. Apart from these, the contemporary folk had a greater amount of time to devote to such labour oriented tasks of bone working. The lower stratum of rural Bengal, particularly the population concentrated on Dom, Muchi, Hari, Bagdi etc. may serve as mobile foreagers of bone working tradition and well known for their leisure. An inclination to enrich the material culture of these early village farmers as well as activities to generate interest in working bone, may create material adornment of their individual status. However, the prolification of life that we observed with our limited collection may not be exhaustive, rather suggestive which need investigation through the scope of further horizontal digging.

Metal objects : Copper and Iron

Sheet Number 16,17,18 and 19 envisages Bar-diagram and Pie-chart of Metal objects. Copper : 59. Iron : 15.

The analysis of metal objects has rendered a scope of discussing the history of the use of metal in Eastern India in general and Pandurajar Dhibi in particular. The frequency of metal objects envisages certain theoritical as well as evidential perspective for the better understanding about the use of metal by early village farming community at Pandurajar Dhibi. The question may be related to a metal or alloy or a non-metal, it's manufacturing technique, source of mine from where it was originated (imported or local), how it was brought and other such details.

Pandurajar Dhibi has yielded a limited variety of copper objects like fish hook, nail parer, bangles, ring, eye-pencils and bead. A flat copper celt with a convex cutting edge has been excavated from Mahisdal. In contrast to these sites, Rajghat and Chirand has also yielded iron and copper objects.

The excavation at Pandurajar Dhibi has yielded 59 copper objects and 15 iron objects. Metal in the form of copper appeared in the life these early village farmers during C.1200 B.C. Period II has yielded 8 - copper specimens of which 6 - belongs to serve as toilet item while the remaining 2 are an ornaments and hunting equipment respectively.

Period III of Pandurajar Dhibi has yielded an increase in the number of copper objects. The noteworthy specimens are bangles, rings, stylus, pin etc. which once again suggest that it's use was restricted in manufacturing ornaments due to its scarcity during C.900 B.C. to C.600 B.C. Occurrence of copper ore probably indicate the local manufacturing of copper objects.

The next period (Pd. : IV), ranging from C.600 B.C. to C. 300 B.C. has witnessed an increase to copper objects. A total of 14 - copper implements included Rings (8 - pcs.), Bangles (4 pcs), Eye-pencil (1 pc) and Pin (1 pc.).

The excavation at Pandurajar Dhibi has yielded the maximum number of copper objects in period V ranging from C.300 B.C. to C. 200 A.D. Apart from the objects, noticed in previous period, the new introductions are spoon, plate and interestingly enough a spiral wire.

Iron appeared in the life of these people during period III (C.900 B.C. to C.600 B.C.). This period has yielded a spear-head and a dagger. The next period witnessed an increase in the number which envisages their use for other purpose apart from hunting. The same tradition continued in the next period, though a lesser number of occurrence suggest it's restricted use.

The proportion of consumption of copper and iron objects according to sheet numbers 16, 17, 18 and 19 clearly demonstrate the limited use of iron at Pandurajar Dhibi. (Period - III. Copper : 12.16% Iron : 2.70%. Period : IV - Copper : 18.92% Iron 6.75%. Period : V - Copper : 37.83% Iron 6.75%.).

Analysis of terracotta objects

Sheet Number of 20,21,22 contained the Bar-diagram and Pie-chart of Terracotta objects envisaging Human figure, Human torso, Mother goddess, Ornaments, Household ariticles, Votive objects, animal figure and a Miniature double edged axe.

The exacavation at Pandurajar Dhibi has yielded a very small number of terracotta objects. Few of them may be associated with some mysterious cult depicting the female figures with voluptous breast and animic look. Occurrence of miniature double edged axe imitating the larger one of copper from Parihati, Paschim Medinipur probably indicate some sort of contact between the early settlers of Pandurajar Dhibi and the maker of copper hoard culture. The object at Pandurajar Dhibi may be used to serve the votive purpose while at

Parihari, it's size indicate towards the cutting of trees. Thus the object prepared and use to achieve a particular desire may change to other form and size by a seperate group of people with some new beliefs.

The human and animal figures appeared in the scene from C.1200 B.C. and continued upto early historic period. Apart from mother goddess, the human figure mainly consist of male torso beside the animal figures of Humped Bull, Dog and the rear half of a tortoise.

The household articles include lid, flesh rubber and a single piece of sling ball beside a bead from period II and a pendant from period V. The pie-chart shows the increase in the number during early historic period.

Analysis of Beads

Sheet Number 23, 24, 25 contained the bar-diagram and Pie-chart of Beads excavated from the different layers of Pandurajar Dhibi.

Altogether 31 beads have been recorded from the site. Apart from terracotta and copper, semi-precious stone like Quartz, Agate, Carnelian, Felsper, Lapislazuli, Chalcedony, Steatite were used for manufacturing beads. Our analysis envisages it's poor occurrence during period I and II while the maximum occurrence took place during period III and IV.

Analysis of Lithic implements.

Sheet Number 26 and 27 contained the Bar-diagram and Pie-chart of Lithic implements recovered from the different layers of Pandurajara Dhibi.

There are altogether 17 - lithic implements excavated from the different layers of Pandurajar Dhibi. Among these implements, ten (10) are microlithic tools while remaining seven (7) are polished stone objects. The microlithic tools included scraper, point, blade and core with the sign of flaking while the polished objects include celt and pestle. The lesser number of lithic objects probably suggest about the existence of an agrarian economy and less dependance on lithic implements.

RE EXCAVATION AT PANDURAJAR DHIBI, BURDWAN, WEST BENGAL, 1984 - 85

The site Pandurajar Dhibi had been excavated previously by Late Paresh Chandra Dasgupta, Director of Arcaeology, West Bengal for four consecutive seasons in early sixties. Due to some anamolis in the interpretation of cultural sequences based on stratification including the problems of introduction of iron, the report was not accepted to the world of archaeologists. Hence a necessity was felt to restudy the sequence based on correct stratification and other analogous problems.

The Director General of Archaeology in India was approached to permit this Directorate to excavate the site once again with a view to achieve the desired result, which was given promptly.

The work of trial digging in three trenches was conducted by Dr. Shyam Chand Mukherji and assisted by Sudhin De, Dilip Roy and Biswanath Samanta. Three trenches (A, B, and C) measuring 4 meter X 4 meter (Two trenches) and the last one measuring 3 meter X 3 meter were laid near the highest point and last one near the fringe of the mound (measuring 200mts x 170mts) at a distance of 111 + mts to the west of trenches A & B. Trench B was laid out about 6 mts to the north of Trench A. The habitation at the site began from a conpact, hard and sticky mottled silty sand and bed rock, composed of decayed sand stone. The depth of the trenches A, B, and C dug out from the surface or top soil are respectively 4.70 mts, 3.75 mts, and 3.20 mts.

The period wise cultural repertory of the reexcavated site is similar with that discovered from earlier excavation. But the co- relation of levels of earlier excavation (1962-1965) and current excavation (1985) at the site is the major achievement of probe in 1985, finds it's place in an un published official report as follows.

PERIOD	LAYERS (1962-65)	PERIOD	LAYERS (1985)
IV	1	V	1
IV	2a, 2b.	V	2
IV	2c, 2d.	V	3
III 3.	3a. 3b. 3c. 3d.	IV	4
III	4, 4a.	IV	5
III	4b, 4c.	IV	6
II	5.	III	7
II	5a.	III	8
II	5b.	III	9
II	5c.	II	10
II	6.	II	11
II	6a.	I	12
II	6b.	I	13
I	7.	I	14

The houses / rooms were built of perishable materials like reed, as evident from the occurrence of burnt clay with reed marks, though no complete house plan could be exposed due to limited nature of excavation. Floors with ovens or kilns were encountered. They were either rammed with kankareous nodules, clay and sand or made of beaten moorum. Existence of deep garbage or ash pit was noticed in the north-eastern section of trench A and south eastern section of trench B suggest that there was a fixed point or place for dumping the refuse.

Thus period I represented a stage when the site was first occupied by a small community who built huts with floors of moorum, occassionally burnt hard.

Period II had witnessed a flourishing stage of occupation. During this period, the inhabitants used to live on the floors of moorum with post holes and reed plastered walls. Some of these small huts contained oven also.

Period III was almost a continuation of the earlier period. Mention may be made of a row of six elliptical ovens, surrounded by thick layer of ash, containing broken sword blade, iron slag and pottery. This may perhaps bear evidence of iron smelting at the site or may be the hut of a iron smelter.

Another important character of the site is the burial practice as evidenced from period I. A fractional burial showing east-west orientation with few potsherds within the habitational area. The number of burial increased in period II. Altogether three types have been noticed among the nine burials. They are : Extended, Franctional or secondary and Urn burial.

Apart from the practice of burial, the material culture witnessed a severe change with the introduction of iron beside microliths, neoliths, copper objects, ivory-comb, in period III when the process of iron-smelting was began at the site.

The earliest inhabitants of Pandurajar Dhibi used ill fired, handmade crude pale red, grey / black ware of thick fabric, showing impressions of paddy-husks in the section. Beside lustrous red ware and Black ware, a new type of pottery appeared in the scene in period II. This type is known as Black and Red ware, and the shapes include bowl with bevelled rim, channel spouted bowl, Sagar based trumpet shaped vase or pots, pedestal cups of black burnished ware, bowl and vase of lustrous red ware are other important handicrafts during the time.

The earlier tradition continued in period III. Sometimes the BRW are painted in white chrome, possessing finer fabric. A gradual coarseness have been noticed in the latter specimens as evidenced by their section. This feature has been noticed in the increased splayed-end of the channel spout. The earlier phase also manufactured a slow wheel turned cooking vessel having enough resemblance with the Santhal cooking vessels at present.

The analysis and classification of painted sherds from Pandurajar Dhibi delineates the existence of 14 types of geometric and non geometric designs. The analysis further shows the absence of these designs in case of incised specimens. The contemporary potters mainly emphasised on floral and faunal motifs during the time of incision. The painting mainly executed on the pot with the help of black pigment though white chrome also occupied 3.70% among the painted BRW and RW. The 14 major types included sub- types of Triangles, Bands, combs and ladder designs. A comperative study of painting executed on the sherds of Pandurajar Dhibi, Mahishadal, Bahiri, Bharatpur, Dihar, Mangalkot, and other explored / excavated sites in West Bengal shows close similarity of designs.

According to an un published official report, placed by Dr. Shyam Chand Mukherji, Deputy Director of Archaeology, Directorate of Archaeology & Museums, Government of West Bengal, after the excavation in 1985, the probable dates of different periods are as follows :

Period I	:	Circa 1600 BC. to 1400 BC. (On the analogy of the excavation at Bharatpur, Burdwan, West Bengal, a C-14, date of period I suggest, C. 1500 BC.)
Period II	:	Circa 1200 BC. to 900 BC. (On the basis of a C-14 date of Pandurajar Dhibi, done earlier as 1012 +_ 120 BC and Mahishdal, Birbhum, West Bengal : Period I Circa. 1380 BC. to 855 BC.)
Period III	:	Circa 900 BC to 600 BC. (On the basis of C-14 date of Pandurajar Dhibi, 1985, Middle level, and conducted by Birbal Sahani Institute of Palaeo-Botany, Lucknow, C. 2580 - 110 yrs BP. i.e. C. 630 BC.)

9

SUMMARY AND CONCLUSION

We have tried to analyse the excavated data from Pandurajar Dhibi and other sites in the foregoing pages. We have also compare the excavated materials of other sites like Mangalkot, Baneswardanga, Bharatpur, Pakhanna, Dihar, Bahiri etc. Unfortunately our limitation in the report of excavation is the absence of information on day to day basis. However, our data base definitely help us to trace the total socio-economic aspect of Black and Red ware Culture represented by Pandurajar Dhibi.

The BRW - phase marks the first well documented chapter of the begining of village-farming settlements in West Bental which was emerged and developed tentatively between 1600 B.C. Hence the work included the material remains of the saidperiod recorded specially from Pandurajar Dhibi and other sites of West Bengal. This phase was first identified in the region by Late Paresh Chandra Dasgupta at Pandurajar Dhibi and since then a large number of sites have been explored and excavated. The overall data has confirmed that the entire early village farming community in Eastern India was possibly homogenous in form. Apart from published explored and excavated materials, the antiquities and potteries, now in the collection of State Archaeological Museum, has been studied to get a somehow coherent picture of the society of early village farming communities and their association with BRW. The main objective of the present work is to write a simple report on the material remains of Early Village Farming Comminities, with special reference to Pandurajar Dhibi. This phase is also termed as Ferro-chalcolithic / Iron Age and our analysis clearly shows it's distribution in the districts of Bankura, Birbhum, Murshidabad, Burdwan and undivided Medinipur. The analysis also tried to describe the behavioural pattern of proto historic society based on Ceramic using hunter gatherer and farming community that relieved on a mixture of both with limited farming. The microlith using hunter gatherer of lateritic Bengal as noticed from the excavated materials of Pandurajar Dhibi and other sites, gradually transformed and merged with the large scale development of the Ganga Valley due to contacts with other regional development.

The introductory chapter envisages some ideas about the formation of early village farming society in India and West Bengal in particular. It includes exploitation of natural resources through the manoeuvering of man power, inter-regional exchange net work, process of behavioural pattern, subsistance economy, religious belief and mode of practice (if any) on the back ground of favourable ecological and environmental condition.

The present day topography and the entire echo-system in and around Ajay & Damodar Valley, certainly had a route in the exploitation history of this regional environment. The physical isolation of these regions have helped the inhabitants in maintaining their premitive character and way of life for a long time. The choice of early village farmers in West Bengal were mainly concentrated in old and alluvial area (Vindhyan alluvium), brought down by rivers originating in the Chotonagpur plateau.

It is very important to discuss about the discovery of BRW- sites in West Bengal on the above background. The mud plastered gobri floor, sometimes washed with lime and the mud wall supporting thatched roofs were the dwelling of these early farmers. The excavation of different sites has also revealed the existence of different categories of villagers. Among them, the farmers, potters, metal smiths etc played the most important role. The excavation at Bahiri has revealed the existence of a work shop, related to metal work and pottery manufacturing. But the evidence from Dihar, Bankura, was related to fishing, harvesting beside pottery manufacturing. It is most unfortunate to say that the anamoly still existed regarding the nature of excavation and information about the general character of BRW-sites and their relationship with the different aspect of life and society during BRW-phase. The housing pattern precisely speaks of some places of living area, cooking place, pottery manufacturing, a seperate place for harvesting & place for domesticated animals. Innovation of new technology, the inclination of metal and the departation of earlier obsolate technology may also evident in our study materials.

Inclusion of the report of proto historic environmental mosaic of Pandurajar Dhibi and it's surroundings is a key to define the distribution of environmental zone in the past. The landscape characterised by floodplains of Bhagirathi basin along with it's tributories like Mayurakshi, Kunoor, Ajay, Damodar and even Dwarakeswar have witnessed the plain land, essentially fertile having a potentiality for any kind of cultivation, particularly rice. Metal and mineral resources played a significant role for the development of surplus in village economy around Pandurajar Dhibi. The undulating landscape of fringe area of chotonagpur extension towards east, not only giving the source of metal, mineral and timber, but also harbour a large number of population in the genes group indicating the tribal, caste and subcaste. Through the process of observation as well as the cultural intercourse between the fringe area and the plain, there was enough possibility of the circumstances to develop a mixed population structure in this region.

The area under discussion is one of the premier region in India in terms of mineral production and for water holding capacity. The soils are of reddish in colour, medium to coarse in texture, acidic in reaction, low in nitrogen, calcium phosphate and other plant nutrients. The climate hardly differs from the over all meso-thermal climate pattern. The modified gangetic monsoon climate in the South eastern parts of the area is characterised by moderate temperature with cold weather.

The excavation at Pandurajar Dhibi established the existence of proto historic phase in West Bengal. The Centenary Conference of Archaeological Survey of India has also declared the site as an early habitation of village farmers in West Bengal. The earlier and later publication on the materials of the site by Dasgupta, Chakrabarti, Mukherji, Ray, Dutta and myself in the Journals, Bulletins, Books etc indicate unanimously it's acceptance as a protohistoric settlement in West Bengal. Even F.R.Alchin, B.Alchin, D.K.Chakrabarti, D.P.Agrawal, Amalananda Ghosh, A.K.Ghosh, H.N.Singh, K.M.Srivastava, H.D.Sankalia and others included the results of excavation and analysis of finding of Pandurajar Dhibi in any archaeological book of India having a protohistoric section.

Though chakrabarti is not satisfied with the report of excavation, given enough credit to Dasgupta for highlighting his major ambition and vision. He want to show the extension of Ganga Valley Culture upto Lower Gangetic Delta.

The earlier stage of excavation at the site has revealed the existence of three phases of occupation from period I to period III before the introduction of iron during early historic period. The site was reexcavated in 1985 due to some anamolies in the interpretation of cultural sequences based on stratification including the problems of introduction of iron. The excavation revealed four cultural period from C.1600 B.C. to C.200 B.C.

The structural activity in Eastern India suggest the use of perishable materials like reed, bamboos etc. The evidence of structural remains from the excavated sites of Bharatpur, Mangalkot, Dihar, Kotasur, Hatikhera, Pakhanna clearly suggest the existence of rural habitation by impermanent materials, supported by courtyards where the domesticated animals were tied up for the procurement of food and other products. They also buried the bones of dead within their habitation floor. The concept of living in a group may existed during this time, but the mode of living has been changed as suggested by the small size of the room, some times circular or oblong. The excavation at Pandurajar Dhibi has revealed various catagories of antiquities. It includes Bone tools, metal objects, Terracotta, Beads and three major types of pottery like, Black and Red ware, Black ware and Red ware. The shapes and their functional aspects has been carefully determined and dated according to our reported materials.

The scope of comperative study is restricted here with the data base from Eastern India. Apart from pottery, the structural remains, evidence of burials, metal objects and their scientific analysis, bone tools and their identification, analysis of floral remains, beads, terracotta objects were studied with an aim to determine their functional aspects as well as comperative study of their frequency for the better under standing about the sites and materials. The morphological analysis of these objects with the help of Bar diagrams and Pie charts along with a brief report on re- excavation at the site throws enough light on the living and subsistance pattern of early village farming community of Pandurajar Dhibi.

Thus a complete, comprehensive and coherent picture of the earliest farming settlement of West Bengal could easily be visualised with the representation of Pandurajar Dhibi. In one hand, the period exhibits a consistency of village life with a mixed economy, which was by and large dominated by pastoralism and agrarian structure. On the other hand, it was the period which witnessed the changing context of technology and social structure. An extended view of such development could be realised with the inner composition of social structure with the survival of village society. During a particular phase, the Black and Red ware assembladge help us to understand the dominance of two social growth viz., Pastoralist (Gopa/Goalas) and Potters (Kumbhakara/Kumor). Aftera certain period of time, our evidences shows the fractional growth of the same social structure. The pastoralist gave birth of another sub- group. Those who were involved in the agriculturein later stage generally indentified as agriculturist (Sadgopa/Casha). Another dominant sub-group bifurcated from the potter classes to extend their knowledge about smelting metal for their survival economy and this group eventually identified as metal smith (Karmakar/Kamar).

The villagers of Pandurajar Dhibi consistantly demonstrate the evolution of that social structure and archaeological evidence adequately subtantiate the above working hypothesis. Our further elaboration of the social aspect of Black and Red ware phases (Early, Middle & Later) could easily be identified with the growth of society by following a pattern of evolution. The incipient stage as well as a period of transition from hunting gathering stage of life to pastoral Sedentism have been observed with the finding of our present study.

The utilisation of nearby resources has been visible clearly among the excavated materials for the enhancement of their economic status. At the same time, the exploitation of different resources forced them to develop their technological aspect. The initial part of this stage never exhibit the importance of metal in daily life. However the period of maturity, certainly incorporated metal in that economic basis. Therefore, Copper and Iron played certainly an important role for the excelleration of their economic surplus, is not more. The structural complex recorded so far having enough similarity with the present day village life of West Bengal. A small housing complex accomodate a few room, circular, square, rectangular or other in shape, mud structure with the plaster of cowdung, rammed floor, periodically polished with river silt, mixed with cowdung and occasional appearance of Laterite, lime and river nodule on the floor, are the basic preparation for the housing Complex. Each and every housing complex is accompanied by a lengthy courtyard, certainly used for their day to day harvesting and farming process including the shelter for their cattle and cow. All these uniqueness and the matter of parallelism could easily be visualise between the excavated remains of Pandurajar Dhibi and the present day remote village housing complex.

The class structure according to the professional activitieslike potter, farmer, metal smith, harder and daily labourers left their refuse to trace the existence of the same. The sophisticated pottery type certainly helped us to know the higher class inside the class structure. Painted pottery also added our imagination about their daily life including ritual & belief. The functional aspect of this ceramic industry speak about their utility in daily life. The storage vessels, cooking vessels and shapes of different types of potteries recovered from the site demonstrate their activity as well as significance of earthen pot in the multifaceted life of contemporary ceramic assemblages which certainly had a route into the ceremonial occasion of the contemporary villagers. In this context, we have further scope of the study of pottery associated to with the consumption of alcoholic drinks, ceremonially or during the leisure time.

The availability of antler and other bone implements or weapons reflect the nature of faunal exploitation in and around Pandurajar Dhibi. The people lived in a favourable climatic condition with sufficient water courses which provide enough acquatic animals as well as the land animals. So the contemporary folks of Pandurajar Dhibi, Baneswardanga, Mangalkot, Bharatpur and other sites of the region were non-vegetarian and clung to game hunting economy for their survival, though each of them possessed individually farm animals. The exploitation reached it's peak during the course of time and apart from fish, turtle, fowl, deer, and pig, panther also constituted the menu of their diet untill the begining of early historic period. The farm animals included cattle and buffalo.

The reexcavation in 1985 at the site in question at Ajay valley has revealed the inclusion of fish, turtle, fowl, humped cattle, Buffalo, Goat, Pig, Hog-deer in their regular diet. We could make necessary inferrences about the dietery system by availing the study materials analysed by Ghosh and Saha in Pratnasamiksha, Volume

I. The domesticated varieties of Pig, Goat and Buffalo indicate that the people had already achieved better knowledge in animal domestication. They had a special addiction to animal protein, as evident from the remains, recovered from ashpit and hearths during the course of reexcavation. They knew the use of fire and used to roast and cook their food. They also depended largely on bone tools for designing and carving the pottery. There were jungles in the outskirt of Pandurajar Dhibi, which harboured a number of wild birds and mammals. The species identified by the Zoologist are mainly of hot humid plains, teeming with vegetation.

The development of art activity in and around Pandurajar Dhibi coincides with the emergence of settled village community based on agriculture and pastoral economy. The domestication of plants became the major subsistence economy apart from cattle breeding and hunting. The concept and technique of pottery has been developed by the contemporary people in response to this increasing man and land relationship. The plasticity of clay which is a major composition of pottery allows it be imparted any shapes or impressions by man. It can be made permanent by firing under certain degree of temperature. In addition, husk of the rice grains, mica and other ingredients were some times mixed with clay as paste, in order to retain extra strength of pottery. It is made at the initial stage by hand and later by wheel. The frequency of pottery types and other related objects clearly substantiate our observation. We have already discussed the material analysis in great details on this aspect. However reinvestigation on such issue may earn more knowledge regarding the economic aspects of village life in Pandurajar Dhibi.

Due to sharp increase in the demographic record and less risk in survival mechanism at Pandurajar Dhibi (Period-II), a specialised group with knowledge of pottery making technique slowly but gradually came into being with the development of more sedentary life at the site in question. The decoration of pottery with paintings, incision and other motifs gradually came into existence has been analysed by the present author in details in Pratna Samiksha, volume I.

The early village farming culture is exceptionally rich for its ceramic industry. However, the nature and extent of pottery as well sophistication is highly variable from site to site, depending largely on the socio-economic condition of the people in each sites. This sort of artistic activity at Pandurajar Dhibi, Mangalkot, Basantapur etc are exceptional in quality and designs, while in some other sites like Dihar, Mahishdal, Bharatpur, Haraipur, Bahiri etc, the beauty and tenor of painting on pottery remain insignificant and marginal.

The site Pandurajar Dhibi was excavated since 1961-1962 to 1964-1965 and reexcavated in 1985, has yielded a plethora of antiquities beside a good number of Black and Red ware, Red ware and Black ware. The Black and Red wares from earlier levels are gradually plain or lipped bowls, where as the lustrous red wares were represented by shallow bowls and vases with carination or elongated stems beside an extended and flat lipped pottery, painted with geometric pattern. This type was also characterised by a kind of simple wheel turned cooking pots apparently blackened by smoke may recall the ageless Saontal Cooking Vessel of the region. The examples of Grey, Red, Pale and BRW, mostly hand made and bearing impressions of paddy husks were found from period I. A change has been noticed in the ceramic assembladge from period II onwards. The appearance of lustrous Red ware with designs in Black pigments, chocolate of buff ware painted in cream or white and Black and Red ware (plain & painted) marked the aforesaid change.

The ceramic assembladge consists of bowls of Black and Red ware having a sharp or blunt carinated shoulder and a bevelled rim or with convex side and a beaded rim, inverted lotus or trumpet- shaped vase or pots with a slightly sagger base and sometimes having a perforations at the bottom, channel spouted bowl occassionally a red ochre stain at the end of cut spouts; the black ware, represented by pedestal cups, the red ware by bowls and vases and a knobbed lid. All these played an important role in the day to day life of BRW phase in and around Pandurajar Dhibi.

Period III was almost a continuation of the earlier period though an elaboration of certain elements and introduction of iron were noticeable in it. The Black ware was most prolific and some of them were incised with crane and a snake, row of fishes, beside the hatched triangles, wavy and prolonged lines, stylised leaves etc. An interesting form representing this ware, included a dish. Bowls and vases in plain Black and Red ware have been found from periods II to IV levels in all the reexcavated trenches, where as painted Black and Red ware vases have been noticed from period II to IV. Painted Red ware vases and bowls bearing geometric motifs in black on both the surfaces from the levels of period I to IV have been occurred frequently. Like wise, painted Red ware vases and bowls bearing geometric motifs in white or creamish white on both or one side have been found from period I to III. During the course of reexcavation in 1985, few examples of Dish on stand and Bowls on stand are recovered from periods II and III. The same year has also yielded Hopscotches made out of discarded Black and Red ware or Red ware from periods II to IV.

Thus the pottery type mainly consist of bowls with flaring rim, vases with outturned rim, channel spouted bowls or basins, dishes on stand, thick storage Jars and Jars with flaring and beaded rim. Functionally all these pottery types served enormous purpose as house hold objects.

Period I according to the report of excavation is premetallic with a few microlithic tools. Two burials have been detected in this phase. The occurrence of rice husk in the core of the sherds is indicative of cultivation of rice in that period.

The excavator highlighted an interval of 200 years traceble after period I. The continuation of microliths using culture and so called hunting gathering economy are quite evident at the site in question. In this context, we may refer to the break because of flood deposit recorded during excavation. The break in settlement along the Ajay valley or the river near by gangetic delta could be treated as an usual affair, the fluctuation of water level through the recede and decede of tidal level along the east coast certainly influenced the flood in the Damodar-Ajay basin. In the recent excavation at Mangalkot, it has been studied that the site also carried the evidence offlood and prolonged water logging in different period.

The composition as well as analysis of recorded material after the break clearly speaking that the site revived with a great intensity of life and rapid change of technological innovation. This thing gradually merged with the process of absorption of metal technology. Therefore the continuation of microliths and the close association with metal technology started the period of transition in the context of technology as well as economy. So the people of Pandurajar Dhibi shifted from Hunting-gathering to farming in a permanent status in one hand and a change of technology from stone.bone to metal certainly helped them to consolidate their lively hood on the other hand.

Copper objects during this phase comprised of bangles open at ends, heavy rings, nail parers, fish hooks, antimony rods, heavy spiral bangles, beads, etc. A few bone tools such as arrow heads, awls, pins, points and harpoons have also been reported from this phase. Apart from this, floors with post hols indicating round, square or rectangular house along with the house materials like mud plaster, reed matting etc have been occurred during the course of excavation.

The frequency of metal objects clearly demonstrate the ratio of copper & iron objects found in different phases of Black and Red ware. Initially the copper objects dominate the begining of metal extraction or the use of metal. However after certain period of time or the component stages, the pattern of the use of metal had been changed. This thing certainly incorporate the events, related to the gradual development of iron technology, though the continuity of Copper could easily be visualised in this changing context.

On the study of the mass of the archaeological materials available at Pandurajar Dhibi, one does not actually get any stragraphic break between period II and III. In fact, reexcavation at the site proved that some of the elements of period III such as complete channel spouted bowl of Black and Red ware, sherds of white painted Red ware, black painted Red ware are nothing but the continuation of earlier pottery tradition and thus could easily be studied in the culture context of period II. The only new pottery that we come across frequently in this phase in Black ware with incised decoration.

The excavation at the site has yielded a row of the six elliptical ovens, surrounded by a layer of ash containing a broken sword blade, iron-slags suggesting an evidence of iron smelting. Reexcavation at the site has proved the existence of a deep garbage or ashpit in the north eastern section of Trench B. It seems that there was a fixed point or place for dumping the refuse was used in different periods as revealed by stratigraphical evidence. A pit has been found in period I level in Trench B, and three pits, superimposing each other belonging to periods I & II in Trench C. Some interesting antiquities including pottery have been recovered from those pits.

A plethora of terracotta objects like beads, balls, bangles, pan-handles, net sinkers etc have been recovered in the course of reexcavation in 1985. Special mention may be made of human head with scratched eyes, seemingly envisages mother goddess. This figure besmeared with black slip, has been recovered from period II of Trench A. Period V level of the same trench has yielded similar type of mother goddess. A terracotta horse like animal with applique eyes has been recovered from period IV of Trench B. Trench B & C has yielded a couple of small shaft with spiral impression at one end (seal ?). No less than eight burials of three types have been discovered from layer number six in period II. They are extended burial, secondary burial and urn burial. The associated objects are beads of Copper and semiprecious stones.

The proposed work coined the term "FARMING" instead of general chrono-cultural term like chalcolithic could be explained in the following way.

Pandurajar Dhibi achieved Sedentism through the process of hunting gathering foreaging economy and the initial status of such development has been recorded during excavation. At the same time, the level which clearly demonstrate the period of development including the transitional phase, exclusively exhibit a slow process of farming gradually merged at the mature phase of village farming settlement. In general, the period have been explained by different scholars as the growth of metal based economy by recognising the importance of metal in the day to day life of contemporary folks. Hence, the published literature explained the material remains of this phase by following metal based cultural society, signifying the importance of metal.

The term chalcolithic has been coined for the explanation of a cultural status of this period. Therefore the entire literature about the early phase of Black and Red ware periodise with a broad label, known as chalcolithic. Here we may explain about the contradiction of such term and the recorded assembladge. In the present work, we have studied not only the entire material remains of Black & Red ware culture from Pandurajar Dhibi but the report of other excavated site like Mangalkot, Bharatpur, Baneswar Danga, Pakhanna, Dihar etc. are also considered seriously. Our investigation resulted in the discovery of more materials for which metal had no role. So the assembladges are by and large non-metal in character though sudden occurrence of metal never signify their utility in the context of economy. The paucity of metal associated data always signify the findings, recorded so far at early stage of development.

On the other hand, one could easily coined the period as incipient stage of farming, mature phase of farming and later development, farming in association with metal has been evident in the excavated remains of proto-historic West Bengal. The justification for the adoptation of the term "Farming" could be substantiated with the fact that the farmers or villagers of proto historic West Bengal achieved pottery technology and farming economy without application of metal for their survial and development.

The availability of a few minor metal object in the form of ring, bangle and other kinds of ornaments beside a few unidentified copper objects could be explained as insignificant house hold objects having no relation with survival economy. The potentiality of such assembladges signify the importance of metal objects in the day to day economy, could only be tested by the attestation of evidence coming from period III onwards around C 500 B.C., if not later.

Therefore the justification of the term early village farming with or without metal, could easily be entertained with the help of excavated evidence from Pandurajar Dhibi and other sites. The discarded theorisation of metal based economy and the term chalcolithic should be challenged in the context of scientific investigation of excavated finds and we have constrain to accept and extend our scope for the visualisation of chalcolithic culture at the early stage of Settlement History in Proto historic West Bengal. The alternative which we propose in this work is easy to accept as it is supported by our finding and equally important to remove the anamoly in the present investigated results.

Plate 1

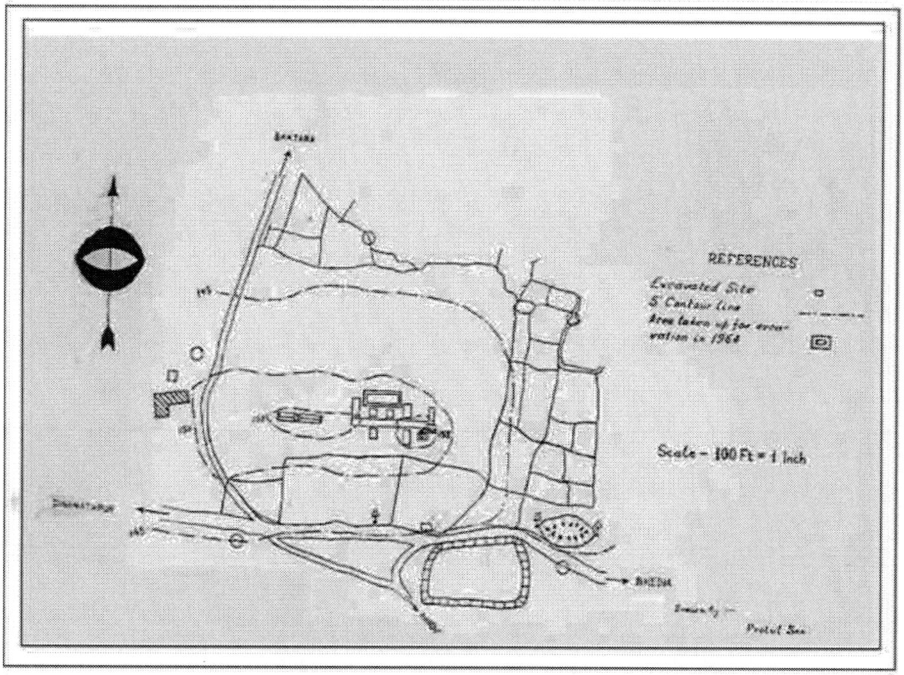
REFERENCES
Excavated Site
5' Contour line
Area taken up for excavation in 1964
Scale – 100 Ft = 1 Inch

A

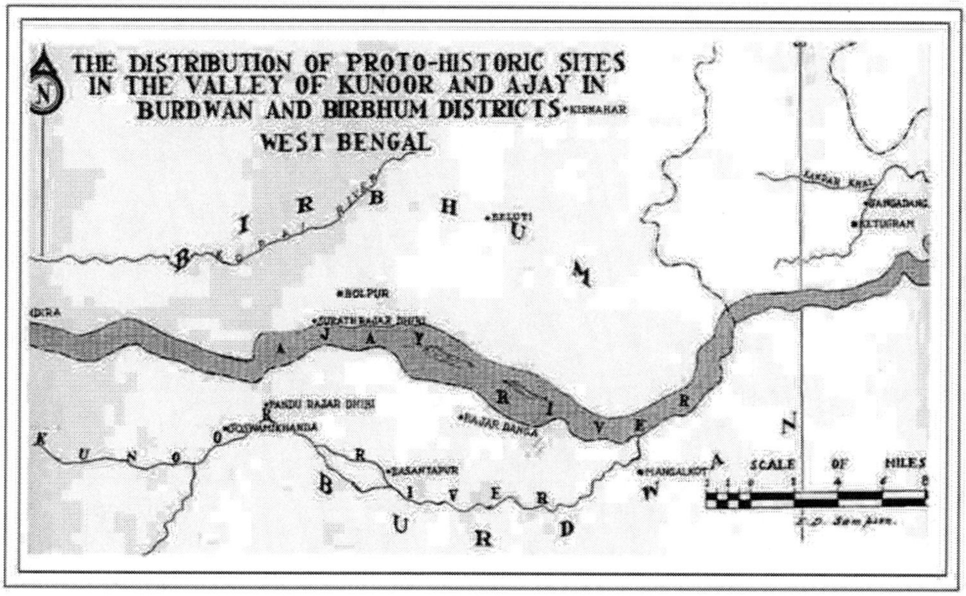
THE DISTRIBUTION OF PROTO-HISTORIC SITES IN THE VALLEY OF KUNOOR AND AJAY IN BURDWAN AND BIRBHUM DISTRICTS
WEST BENGAL
N
B I R B H U M
BOLPUR
A J A Y R I V E R
PANDU RAJAR DHIBI
RAJAR DANGA
BASANTAPUR
MANGALKOT
K U N O O R R I V E R
B U R D W A N
SCALE OF MILES

B

Plate 2

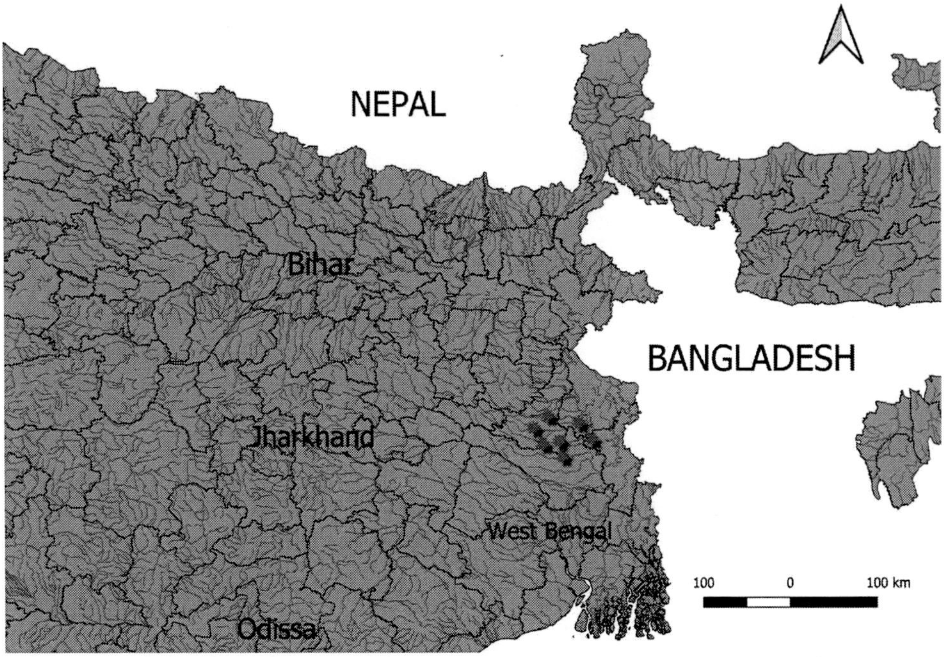
NEPAL
Bihar
BANGLADESH
Jharkhand
West Bengal
Odissa
100 0 100 km

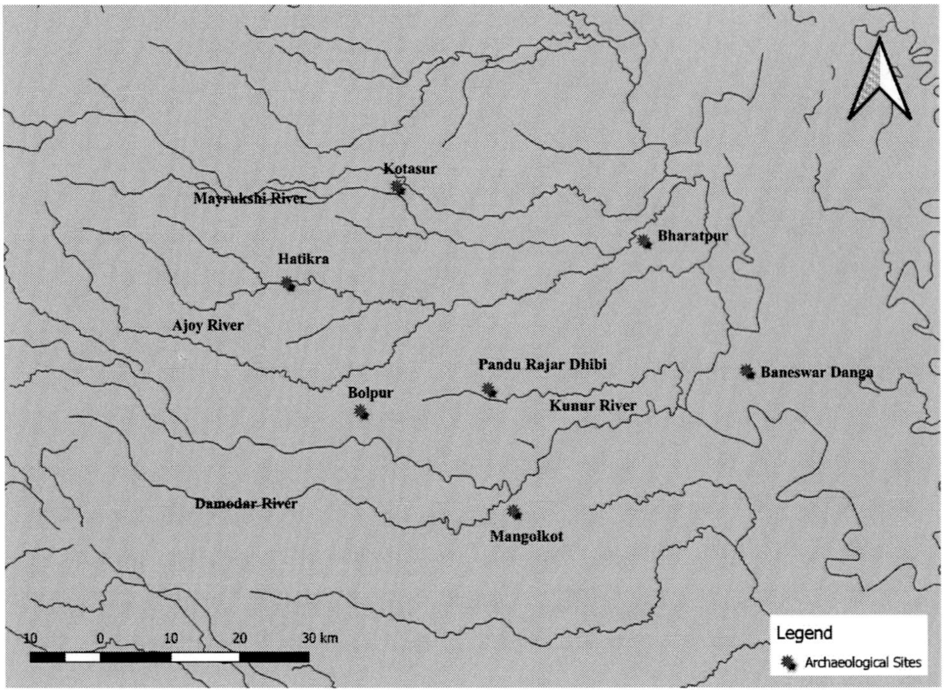
Kotasur
Mayrukshi River
Bharatpur
Hatikra
Ajoy River
Pandu Rajar Dhibi
Baneswar Danga
Bolpur
Kunur River
Damodar River
Mangolkot
10 0 10 20 30 km
Legend
Archaeological Sites

Plate 3

A

B

Plate 4

A

B

Plate 5

A

B

Plate 6

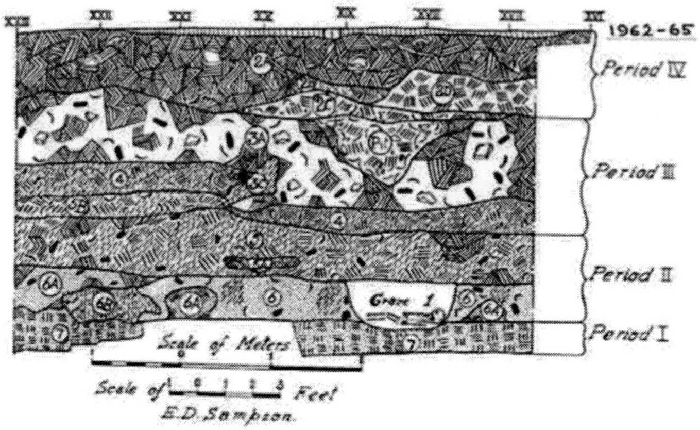

The northern Section of Trench No. IC. This is a partial view of the entire northern section as stratified during excavation at Pandu Rajar Dhibi in 1963.

1985	1962-65	1985
①	Layer (1)—Surface humus grayish loose soil containing *kankar* and sand.	Pd-V
②	Layer (2A)—Compact grayish brown soil full of brickbats. Layer (2B)—Compact grayish soil with ash, charcoal, potsherds and nodules of brickbats.	
③	Layer (2C)—Slightly loose grayish earth with potsherds and nodules of brickbats. Layer (2D)—Slightly loose earth with few brick-bats. The patch belongs to rubble-pavement. Pit by (2C)	
④	Layer (3A)—Less compact brownish earth with potsherds and brickbats. Layer (3C)—Patch of ash with fragments of pottery.	Pd-IV
⑤ + ⑥	Layer (4)—Loose sooty gray sandy soil with scattered mottles.	
⑦	Layer (5)—Greenish white loose earth with ash, charcoal and patches of slightly compact earth.	Pd-III
⑧ ⑨	Layer (5A)—A thin patch of burnt earth. Sherds.	
⑩ ⑪	Layer (6)—Buffish silty sand with occurrence of mottles and scanty remains of ash, charcoal and pot-sherds.	Pd-II
⑫	Layer (6A)—Silty sand with charcoal and patches of slightly compact earth mixed with ash.	Pd-I
⑬	Layer (6B)—Loose earth of dark gray colour with dots of charcoal, ashes and fragments of pottery.	
⑭	Layer (7)—Compact mottled silty sand. Layers of Periods I & II revealed human cemetery.	

SECTION SHOWING THE CORELATION OF LAYERS & PHASES BETWEEN EARLIER & LATER EXCAVATION AT PANDURAJAR DHIBI. (AFTER DASGUPTA:1964)

Plate 7

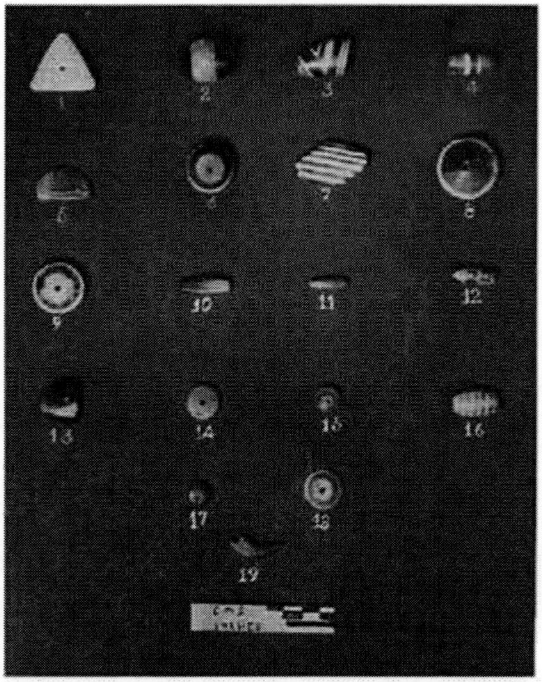

A

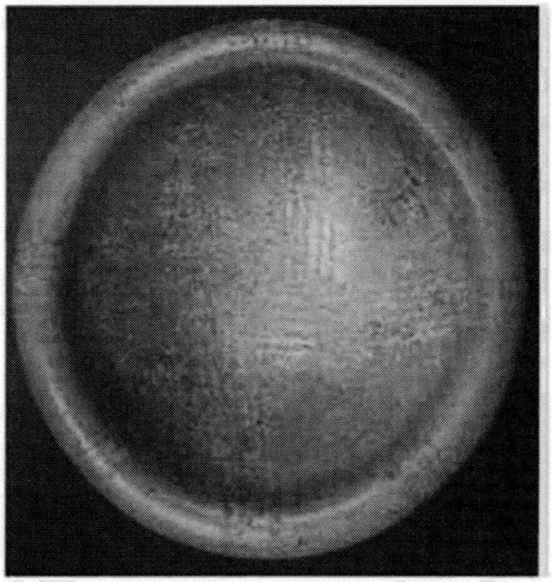

B

Plate 8

PHOTOGRAPH- RANJIT SEN

Plate 9

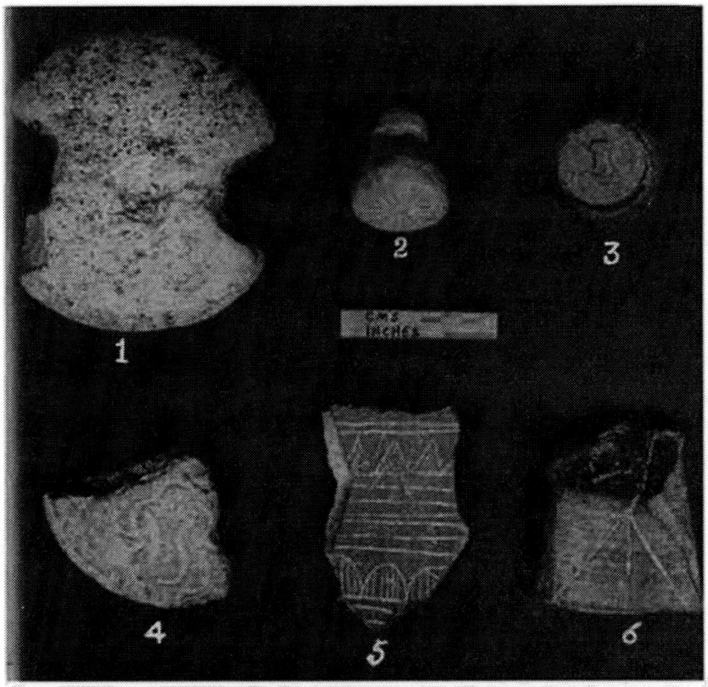

POTTERY TERRACOTTA SEAL -SEALING,VOTIVE AXE EXCAVATED FROM PANDURAJAR DHIBI,1964

HAND MADE & WHEEL MADE POT SHARDS ,PRD

Plate 10

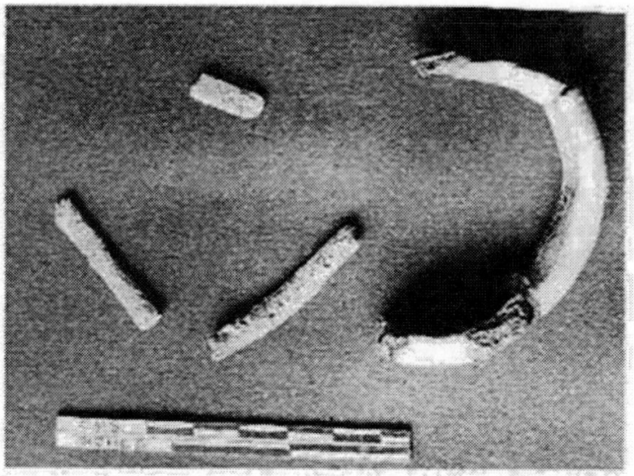

FRAGMENTS OF COPPER BANGLES:PANDURAJAR DHIBI

FRAGMENT OF RINGSTON :PANDURAJAR DHIBI

IRON OBJECTS :PANDURAJAR DHIBI

Plate 11

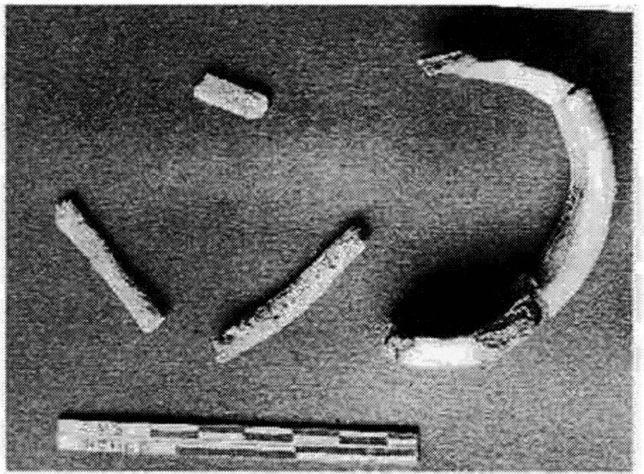

FRAGMENTS OF COPPER BANGLES:PANDURAJAR DHIBI

FRAGMENT OF RINGSTON :PANDURAJAR DHIBI

IRON OBJECTS :PANDURAJAR DHIBI

Plate 12

TERRACOTTA BULL: PANDURAJAR DHIBI

Plate 13

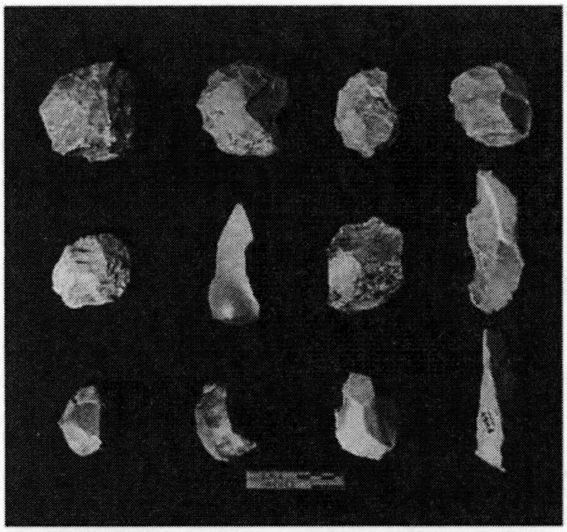

MICROLITHS FROM PANDURAJAR DHIBI.

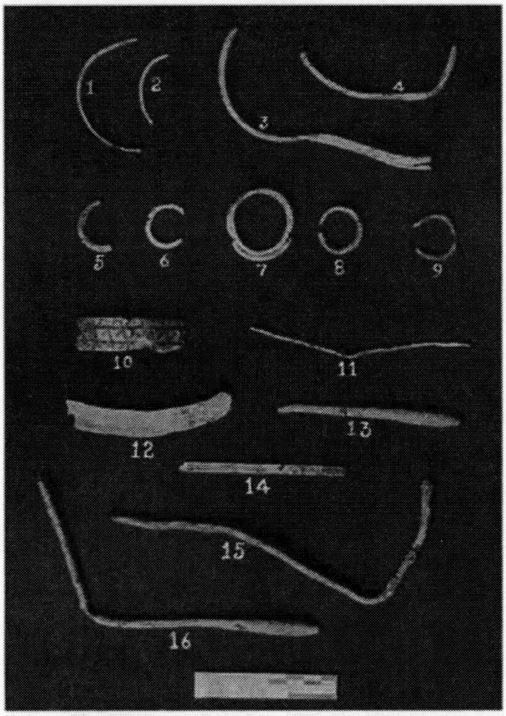

COPPER OBJECTS FROM PANDURAJAR DHIBI.

Plate 14

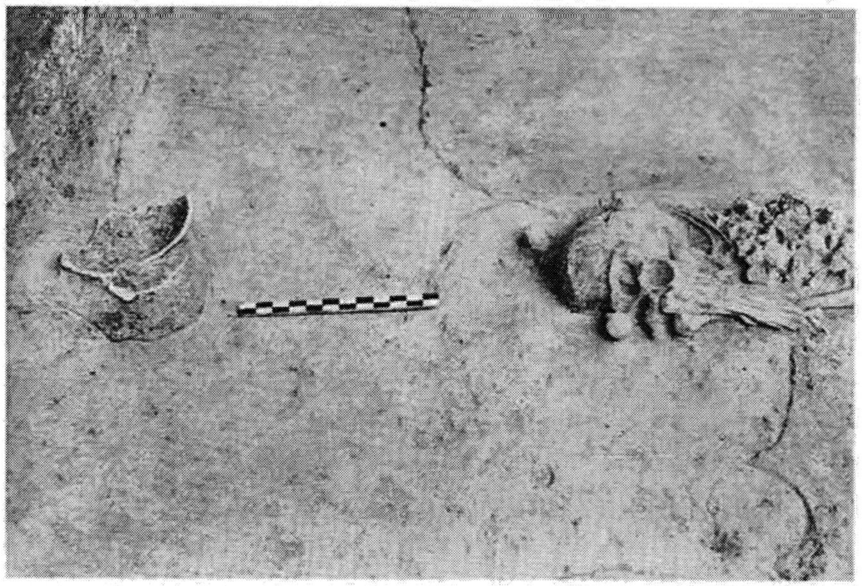

SECONDARY BURIAL .CEMETERY AREA OF PERIOD II PANDURAJAR DHIBI: 1963

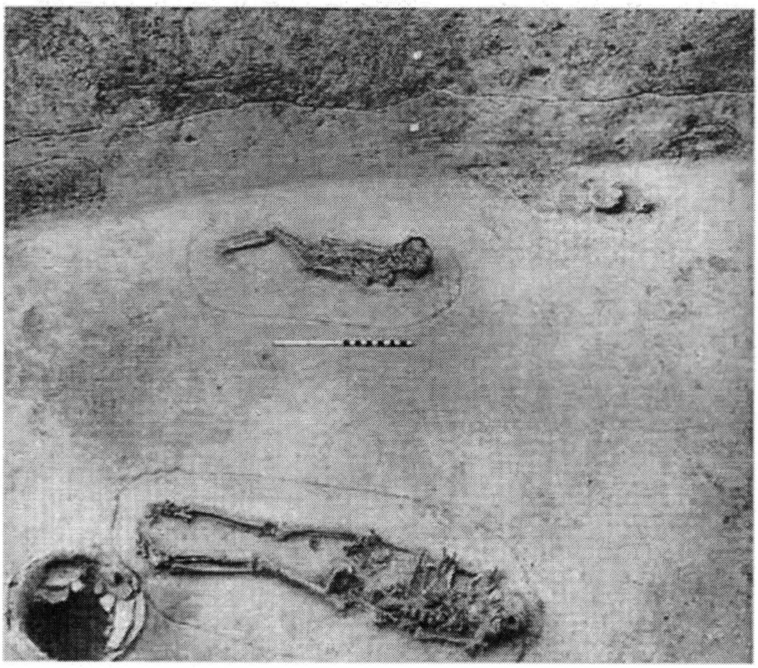

A VIEW OF HUMAN CEMETERY OF PANDURAJAR DHIBI ,PERIOD -II :1963.

Plate 15

A close view of Urn Burial after removal of his lid of Black and Red Ware .Cemetery area of Period -II of Pandu Rajar Dhibi excavation 1963. (After Das Gupta: 1964)

A partial view of the excavation at Pandurajar Dhibi in 1964 revealing period II &III.(After Das Gupta 1964)

Plate 16

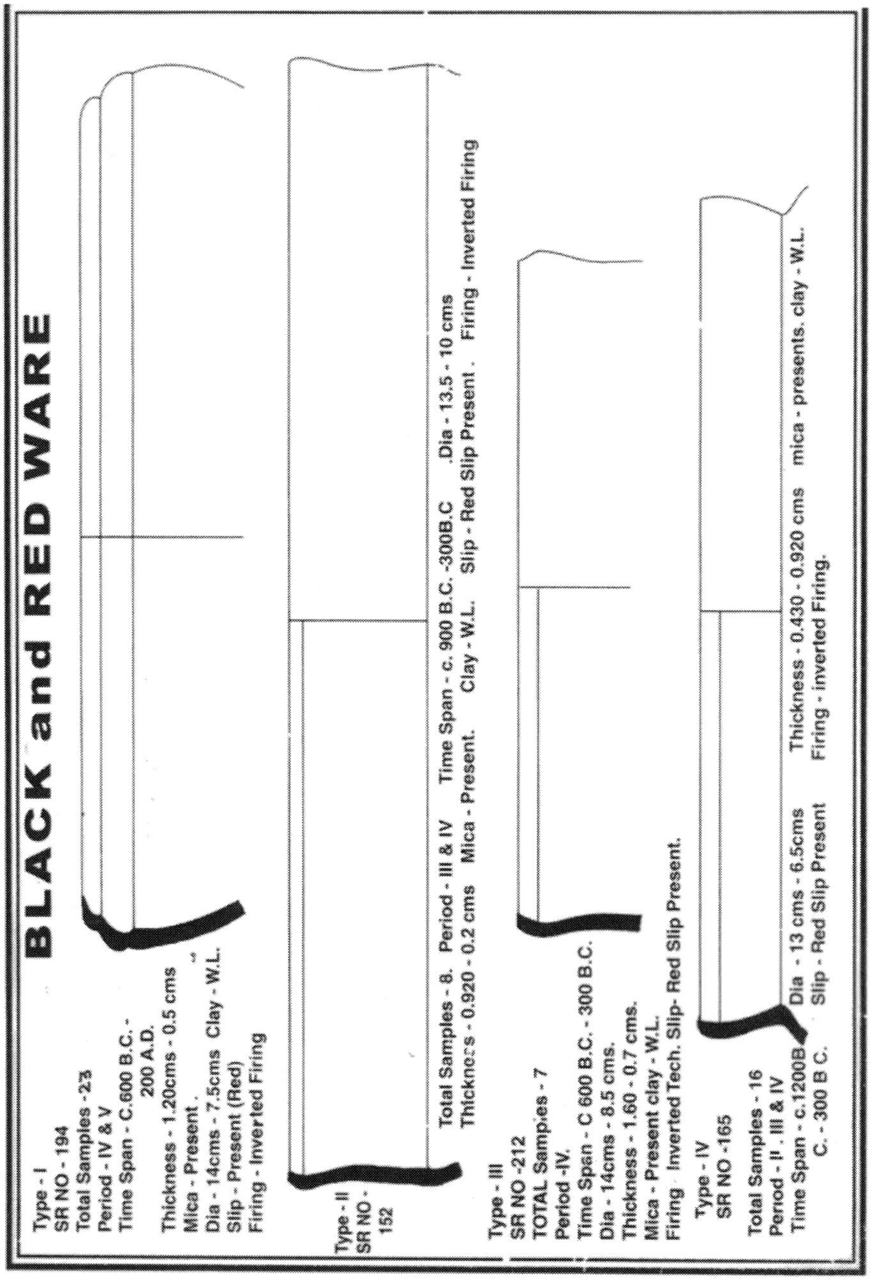
BLACK and RED WARE
Type - I
SR NO - 194
Total Samples -23
Period - IV & V
Time Span - C.600 B.C. - 200 A.D.
Thickness - 1.20cms - 0.5 cms
Mica - Present .
Dia - 14cms - 7.5cms Clay - W.L.
Slip - Present (Red)
Firing - Inverted Firing
Type - II
SR NO - 152
Total Samples - 8. Period - III & IV Time Span - c. 900 B.C. -300B.C .Dia - 13.5 - 10 cms
Thickness - 0.920 - 0.2 cms Mica - Present. Clay - W.L. Slip - Red Slip Present . Firing - Inverted Firing
Type - III
SR NO -212
TOTAL Samples - 7
Period -IV.
Time Span - C 600 B.C. - 300 B.C.
Dia - 14cms - 8.5 cms.
Thickness - 1.60 - 0.7 cms.
Mica - Present clay - W.L.
Firing Inverted Tech. Slip- Red Slip Present.
Type - IV
SR NO -165
Total Samples - 16
Period - II . III & IV
Time Span - c.1200B. C. - 300 B C.
Dia - 13 cms - 6.5cms Thickness - 0.430 - 0.920 cms mica - presents. clay - W.L.
Slip - Red Slip Present Firing - inverted Firing.

Plate 17

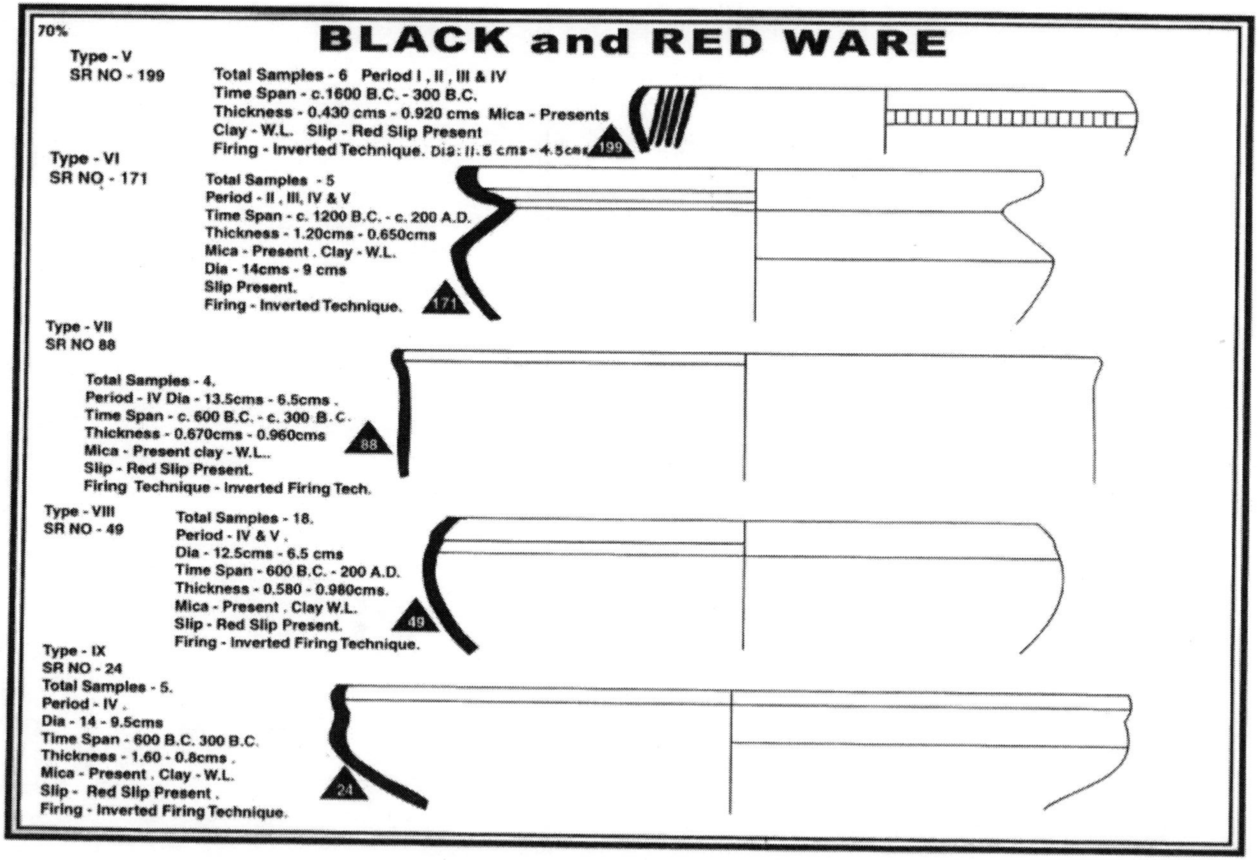
70%
BLACK and RED WARE
Type - V
SR NO - 199
Total Samples - 6 Period I , II , III & IV
Time Span - c.1600 B.C. - 300 B.C.
Thickness - 0.430 cms - 0.920 cms Mica - Presents
Clay - W.L. Slip - Red Slip Present
Firing - Inverted Technique. Dia: 11.5 cms - 4.5cms
199
Type - VI
SR NO - 171
Total Samples - 5
Period - II , III, IV & V
Time Span - c. 1200 B.C. - c. 200 A.D.
Thickness - 1.20cms - 0.650cms
Mica - Present . Clay - W.L.
Dia - 14cms - 9 cms
Slip Present.
Firing - Inverted Technique.
171
Type - VII
SR NO 88
Total Samples - 4.
Period - IV Dia - 13.5cms - 6.5cms .
Time Span - c. 600 B.C. - c. 300 B.C.
Thickness - 0.670cms - 0.960cms
Mica - Present clay - W.L.
Slip - Red Slip Present.
Firing Technique - Inverted Firing Tech.
88
Type - VIII
SR NO - 49
Total Samples - 18.
Period - IV & V .
Dia - 12.5cms - 6.5 cms
Time Span - 600 B.C. - 200 A.D.
Thickness - 0.580 - 0.980cms.
Mica - Present . Clay W.L.
Slip - Red Slip Present.
Firing - Inverted Firing Technique.
49
Type - IX
SR NO - 24
Total Samples - 5.
Period - IV .
Dia - 14 - 9.5cms
Time Span - 600 B.C. 300 B.C.
Thickness - 1.60 - 0.8cms .
Mica - Present . Clay - W.L.
Slip - Red Slip Present .
Firing - Inverted Firing Technique.
24

Plate 18

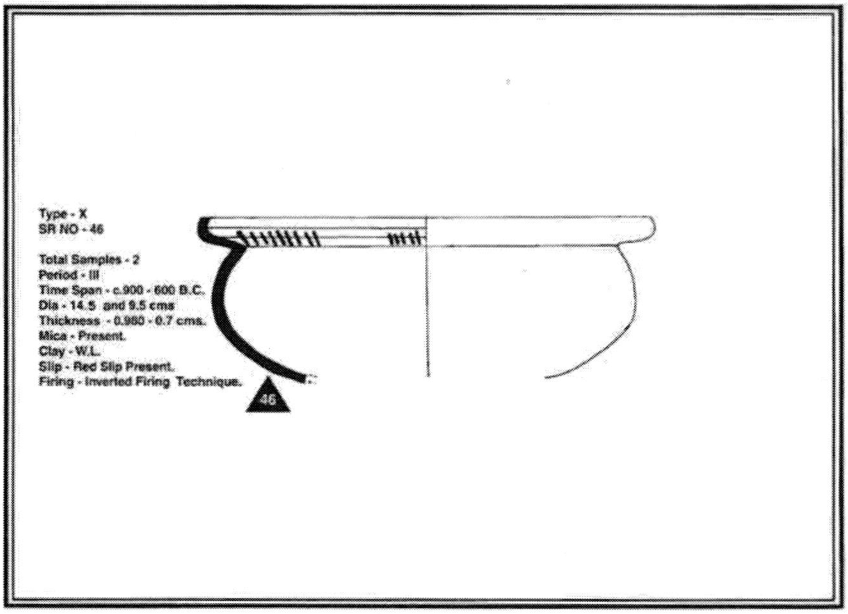

Plate 19

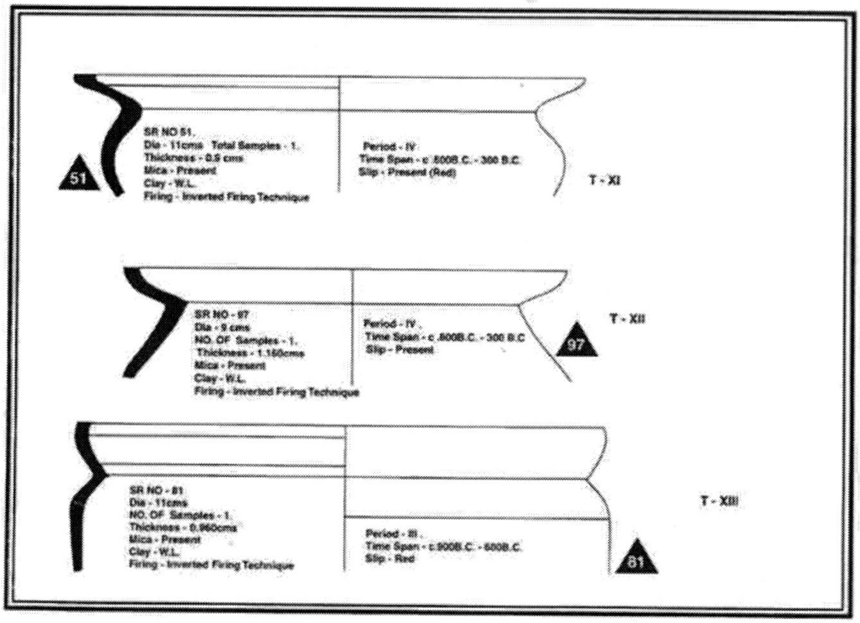

Plate 20

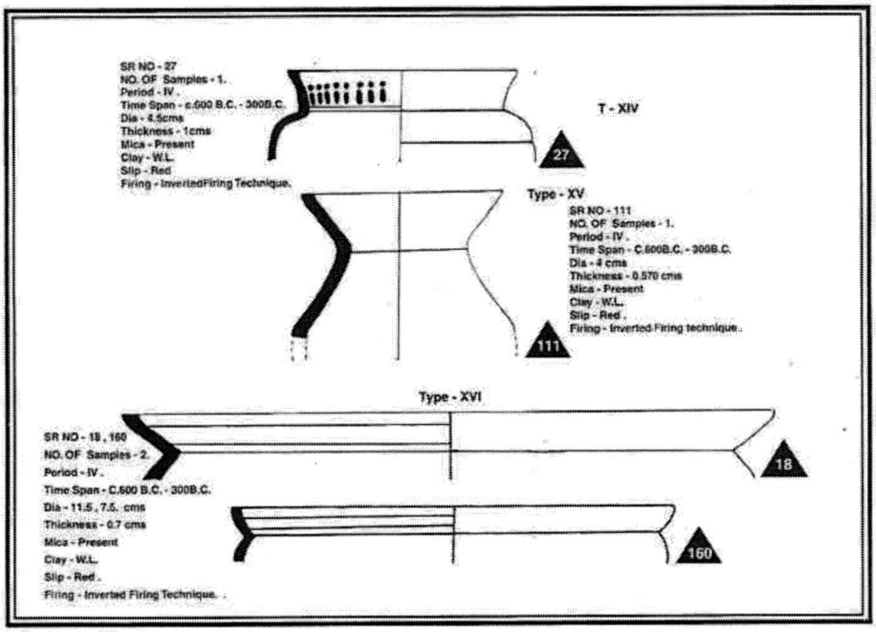

Plate 21

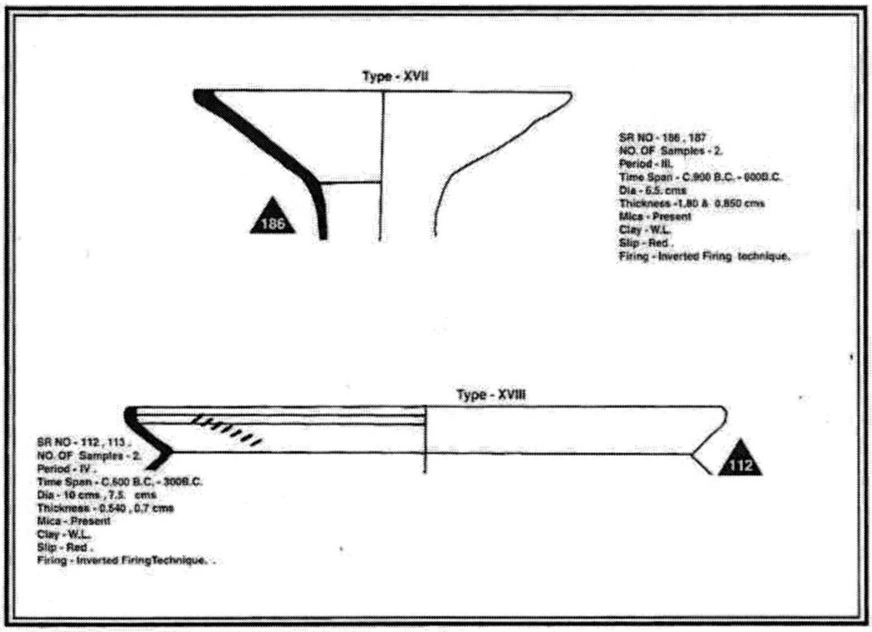

Plate 22

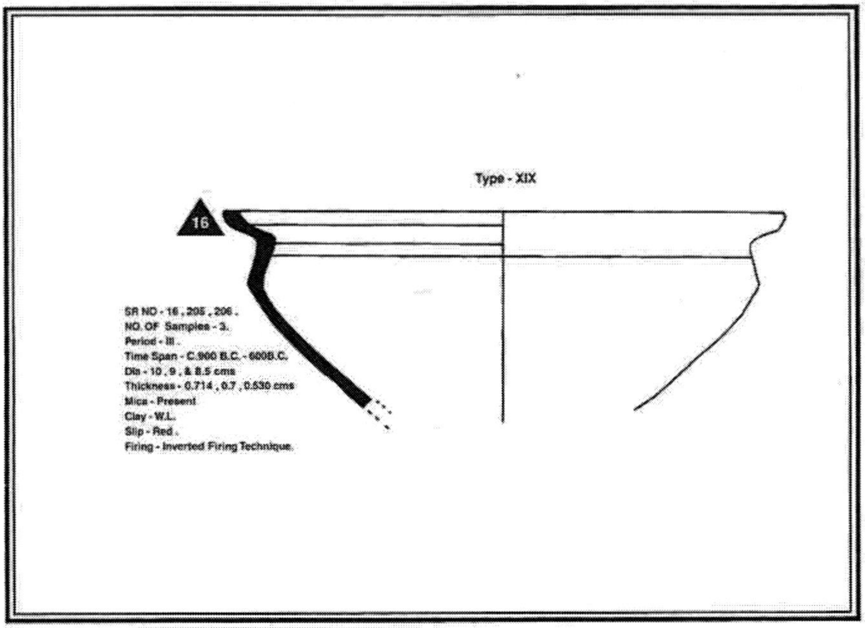

Plate 23

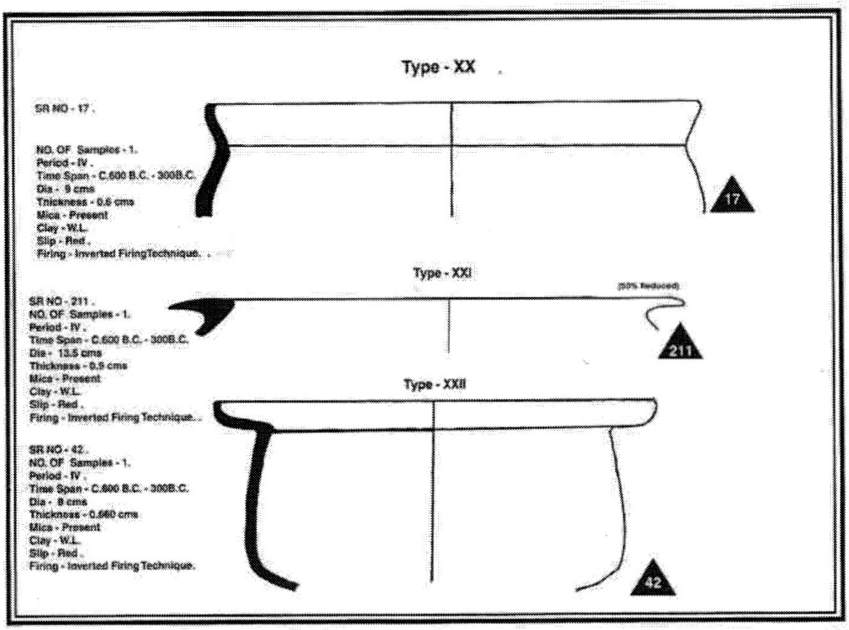

Plate 24

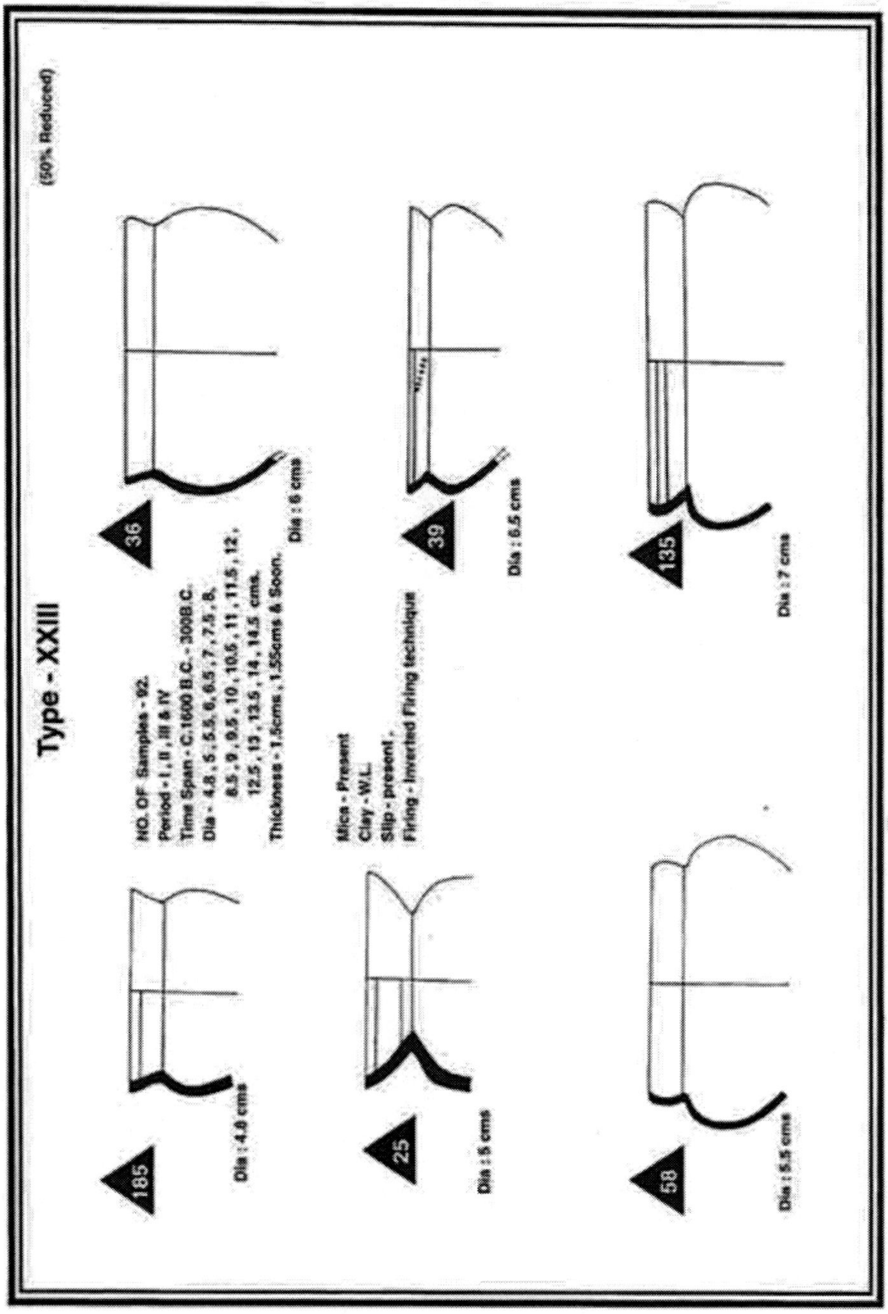
(50% Reduced)
Type - XXIII
NO. OF Samples - 92.
Period - I, II, III & IV
Time Span - C.1600 B.C. - 300B.C.
Dia - 4.8, 5, 5.5, 6, 6.5, 7, 7.5, 8, 8.5, 9, 9.5, 10, 10.5, 11, 11.5, 12, 12.5, 13, 13.5, 14, 14.5 cms.
Thickness - 1.5cms, 1.55cms & Soon.
Mica - Present
Clay - W.L.
Slip - present ,
Firing - Inverted Firing technique
185
Dia : 4.8 cms
36
Dia : 6 cms
25
Dia : 5 cms
39
Dia : 6.5 cms
58
Dia : 5.5 cms
135
Dia : 7 cms

Plate 25

BLACK & RED WARE

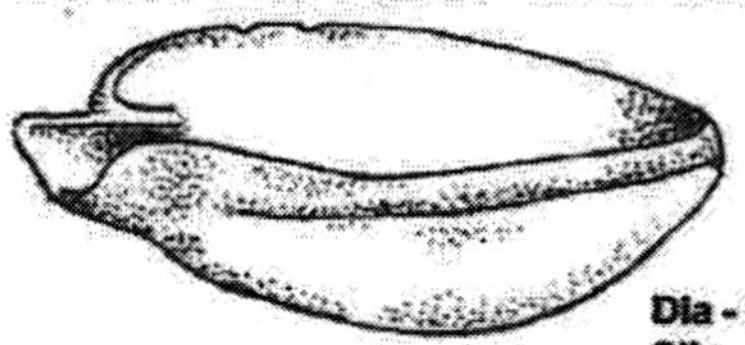

Type - 24.SR. NO. - 238
Total Samples - 35
Period - II, III, 1V.
Time Span - C. 1200 B.C. - C.300 B.C.
Thickness - 0.5 Cms.

Dia - 10.5Cms.
Slip - Red Slip applied on the exterior surface.
Clay - W,L.
Technique - Inverted Firing

BLACK WARE

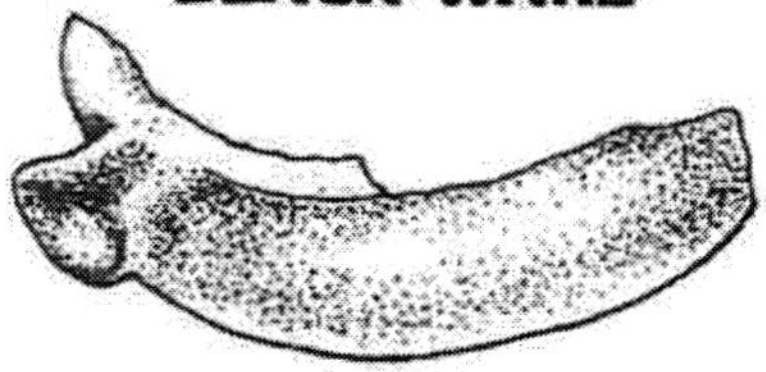

Type –28. Total Sample
Serial No. - 99 to 105
Period - III, IV
Time Span - C.900 B.C. - C. 300 B.C.
Dia - 13 Cms.
(Max Brath of the Channel : 3.3 Cms. 4 Cms.)
Mica - Present
Clay - W.L.
Slip - Block Slip applied on both the surface.

RED WARE

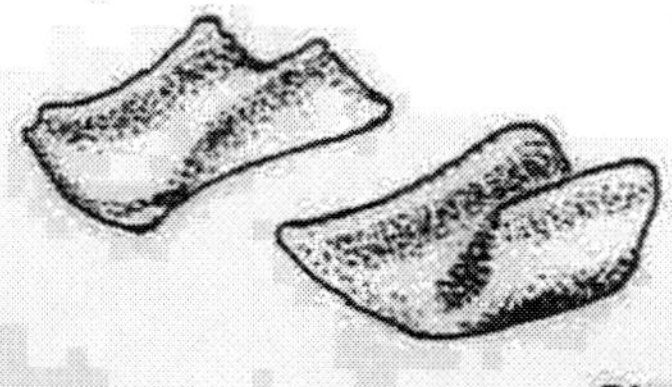

T.18
SSL.NO-35,36
Total Samples - 2
Period-IV, Time Span - C.600B.C.-C.300B.C.

Dia-Not possible to measure.
Thickness - 0.7, 1 Cm.
Mica - Present. Clay-W.L.
Slip - Red Slip on both the surface.

Plate 26

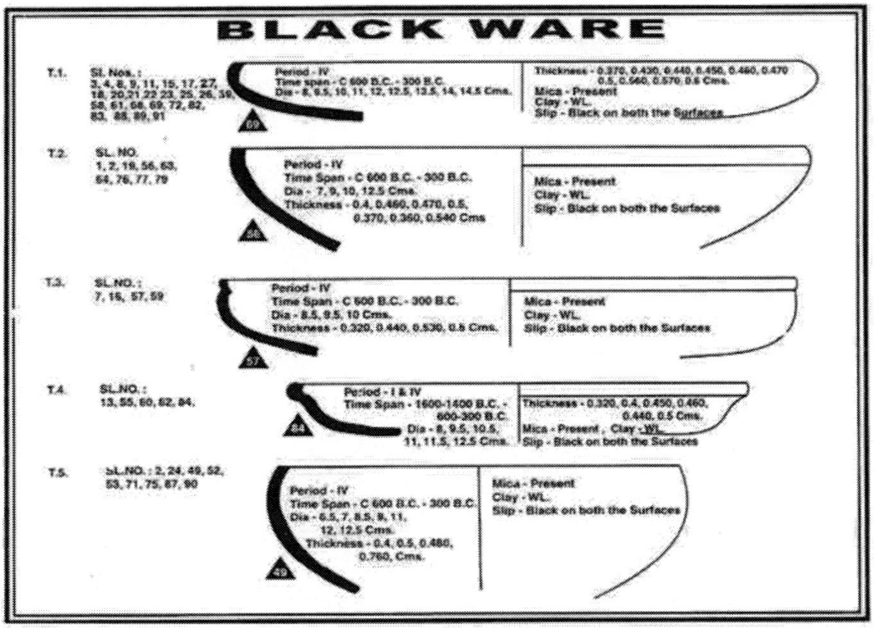

Plate 27

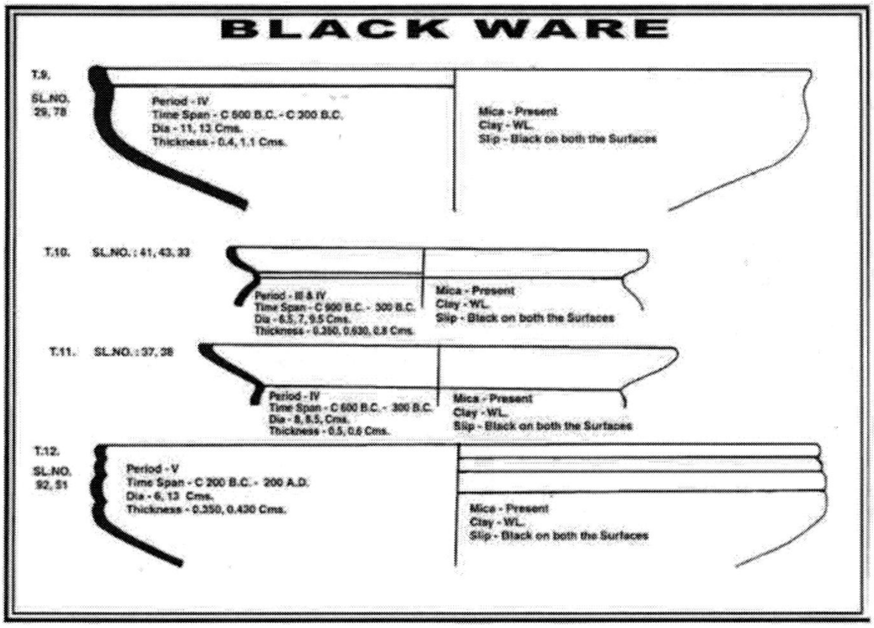

Plate 28

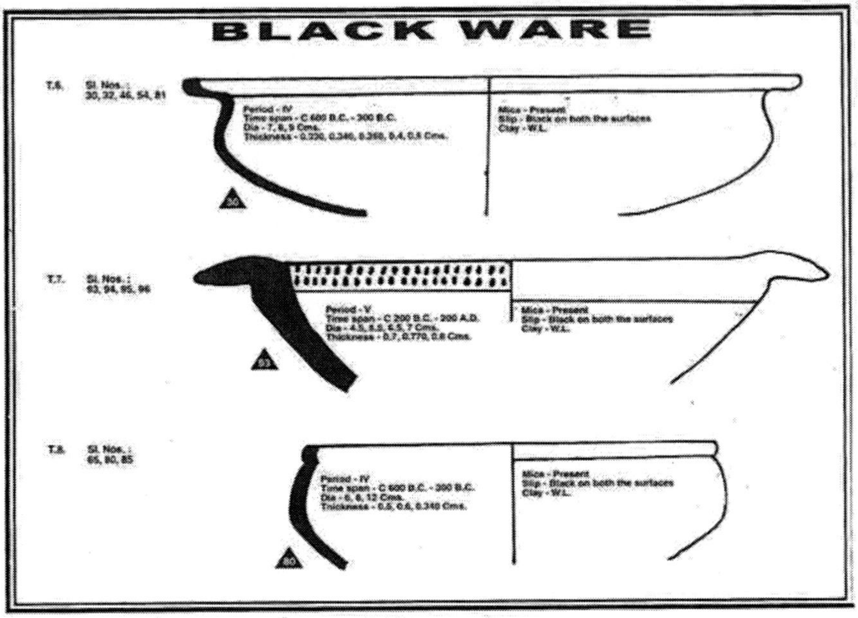

Plate 29

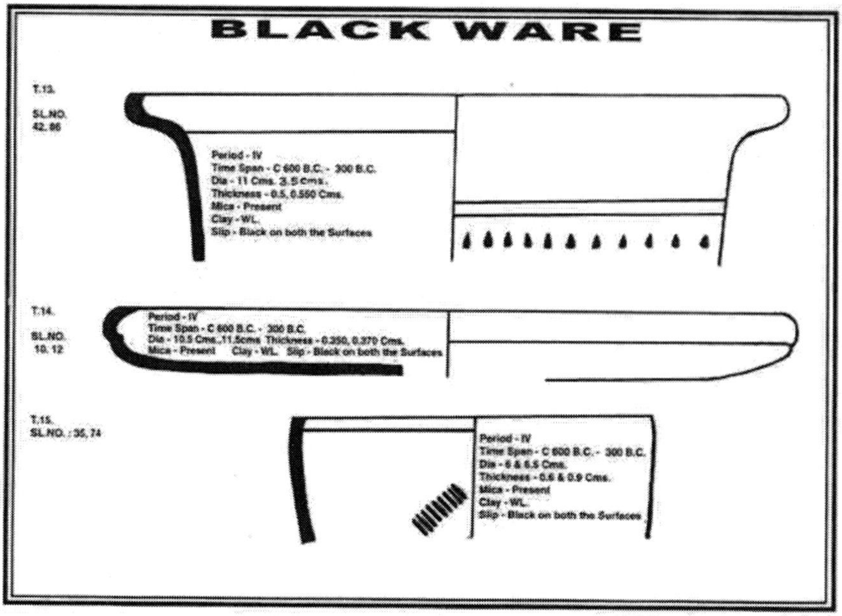

Plate 30

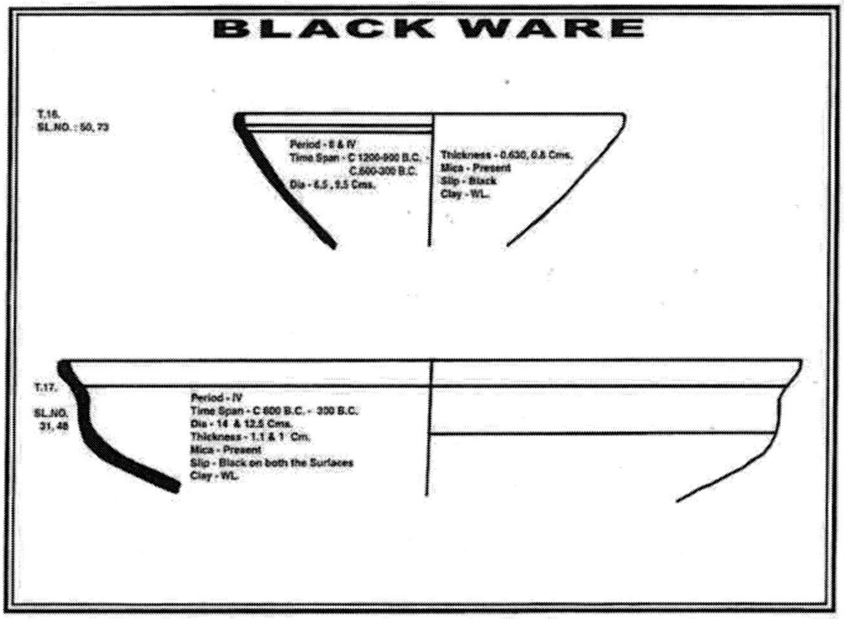

Plate 31

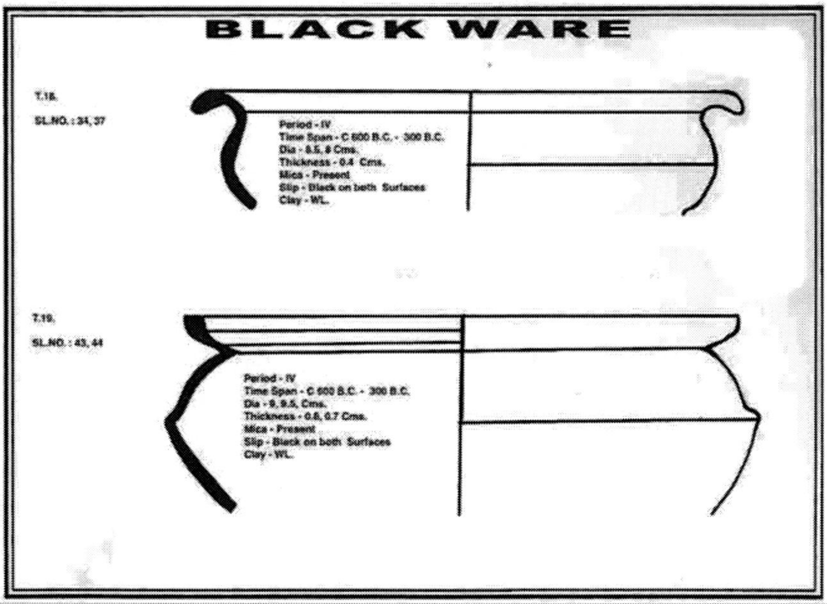

Plate 32

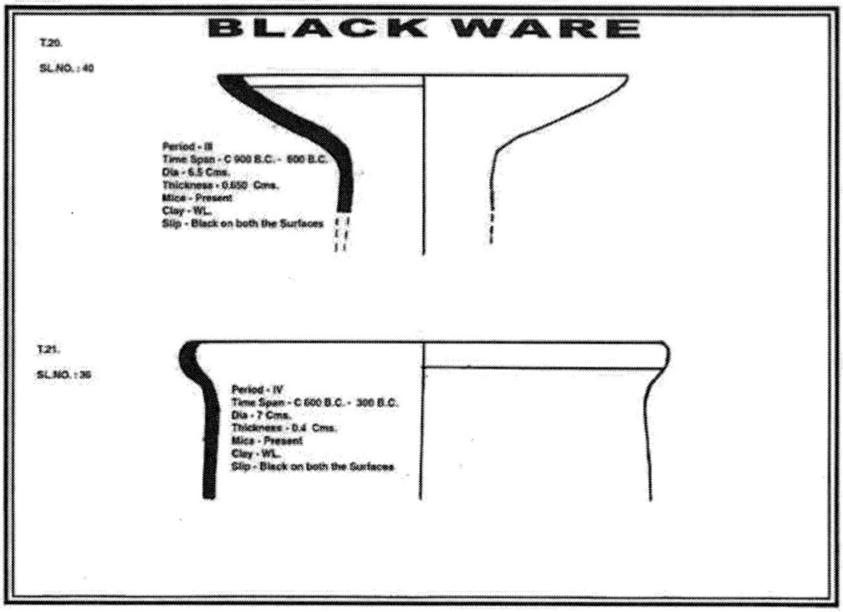

Plate 33

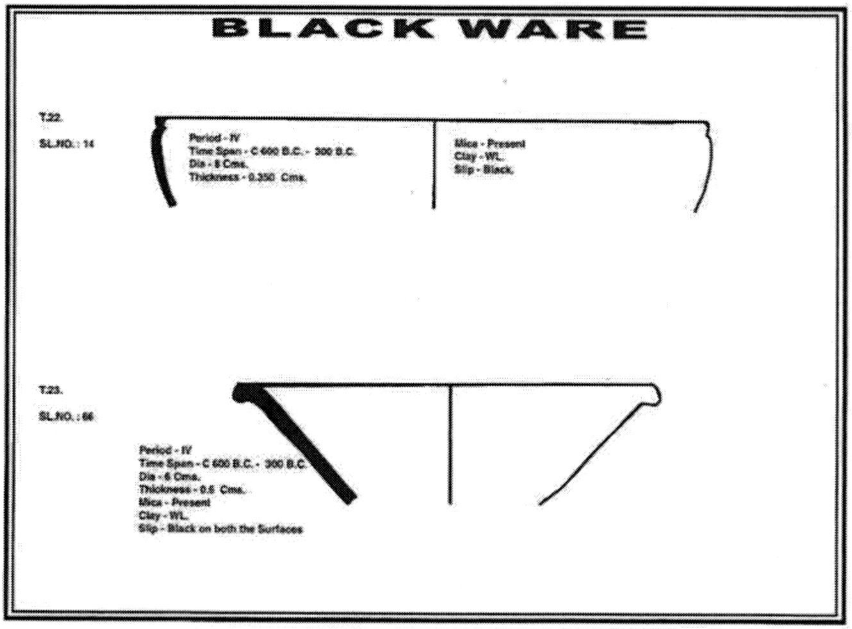

Plate 34

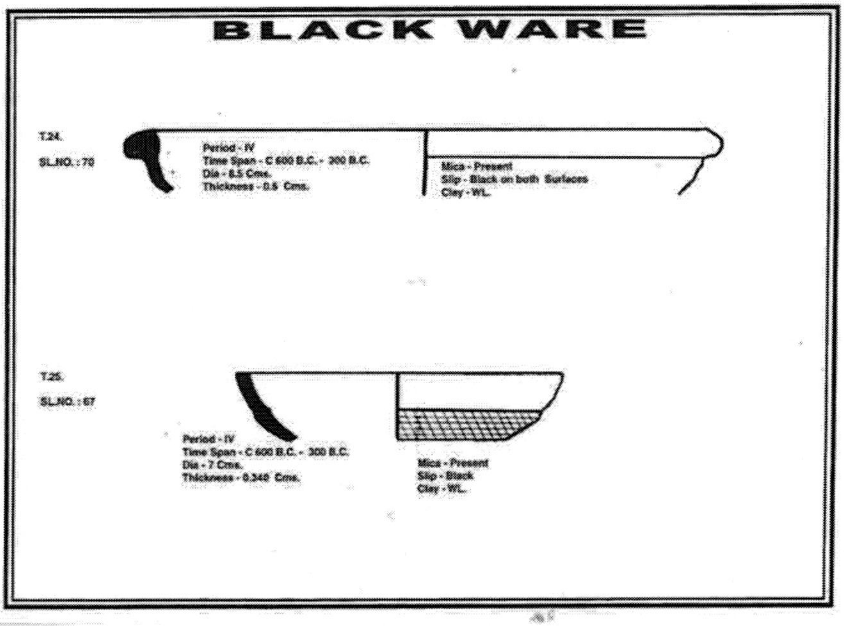

Plate 35

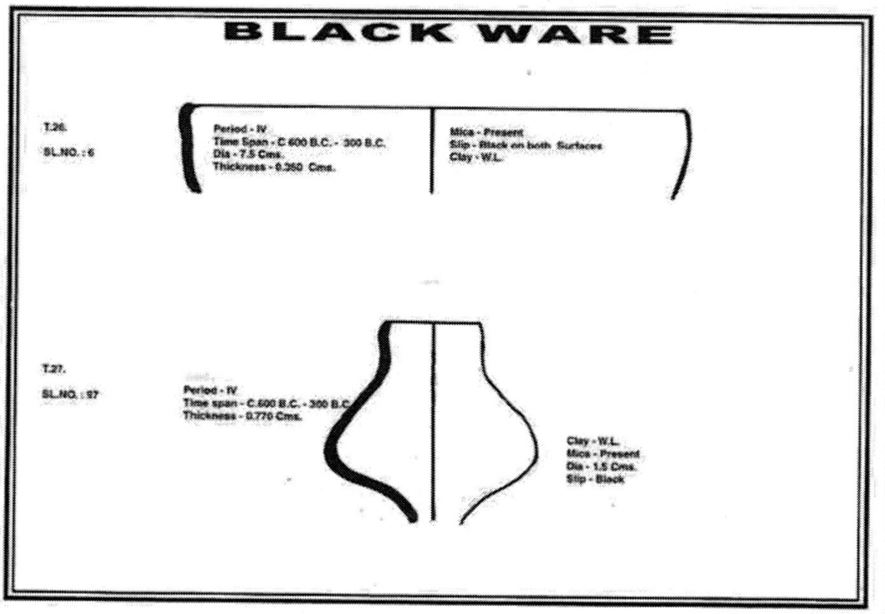

Plate 36

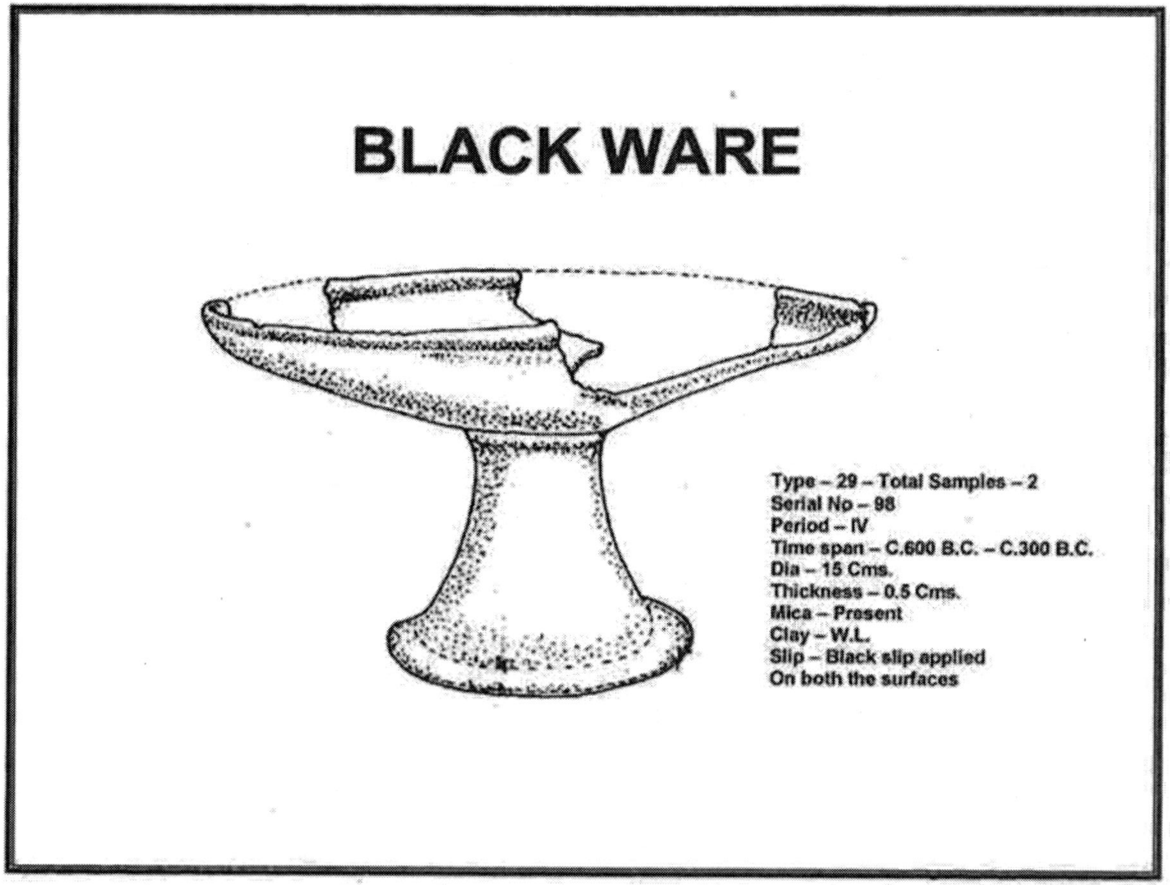
BLACK WARE
Type – 29 – Total Samples – 2
Serial No – 98
Period – IV
Time span – C.600 B.C. – C.300 B.C.
Dia – 15 Cms.
Thickness – 0.5 Cms.
Mica – Present
Clay – W.L.
Slip – Black slip applied
On both the surfaces

Plate 37

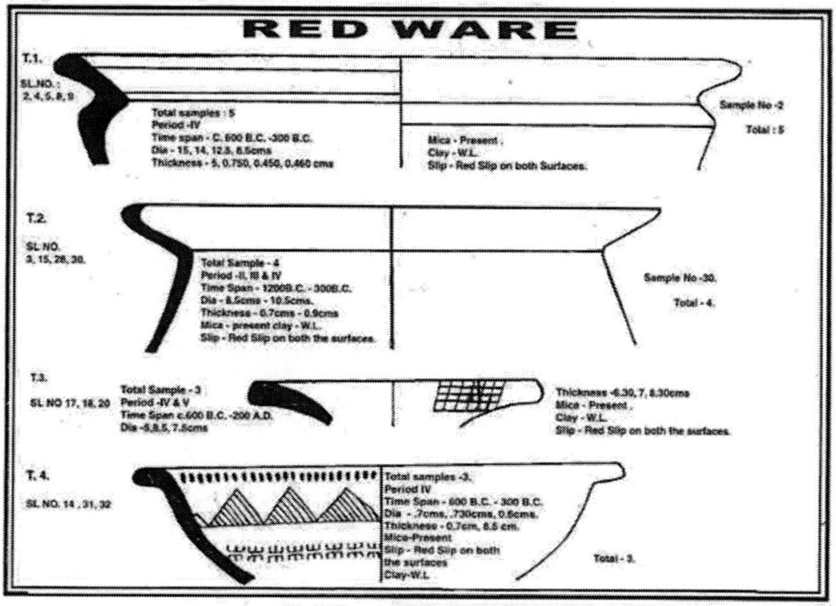

Plate 38

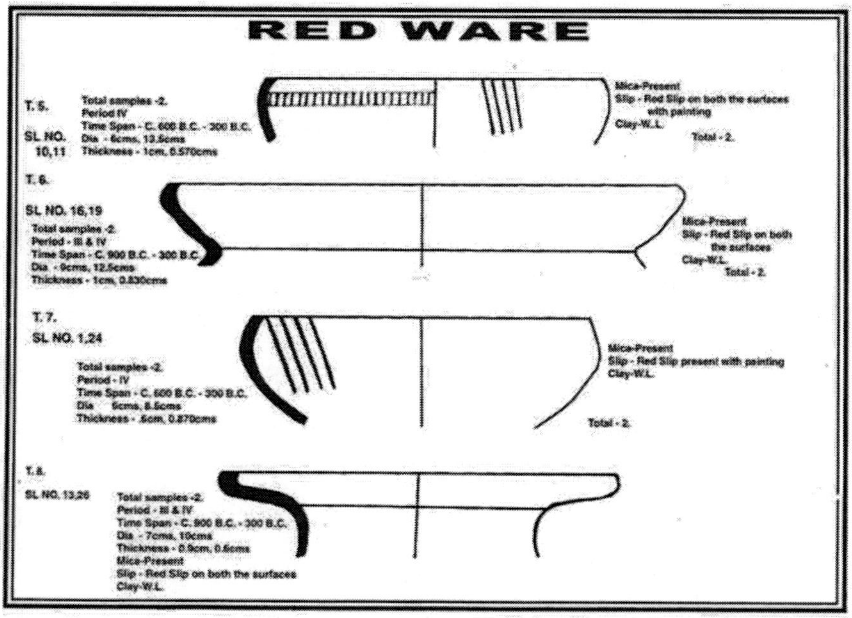

Plate 39

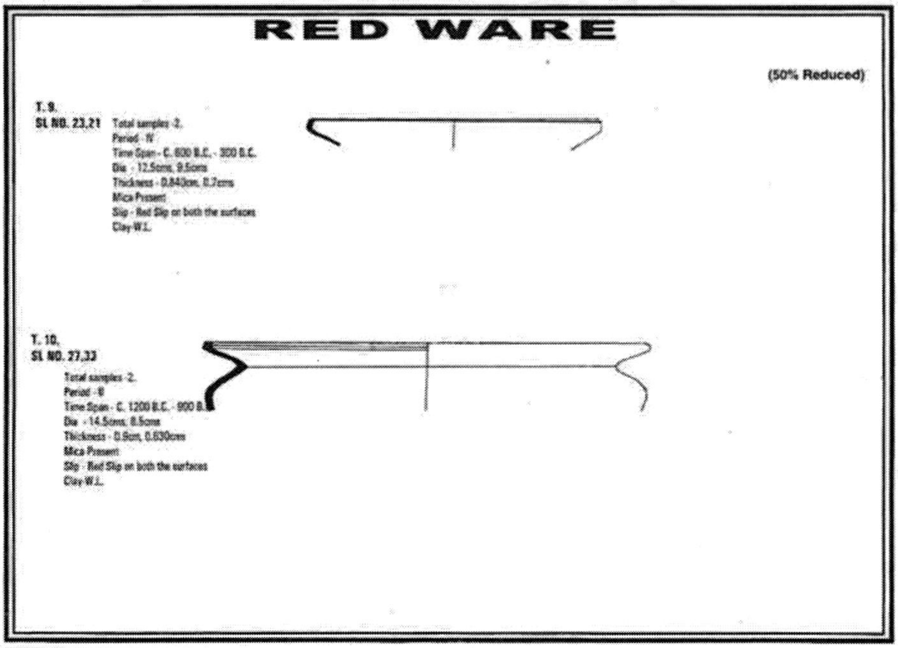

Plate 40

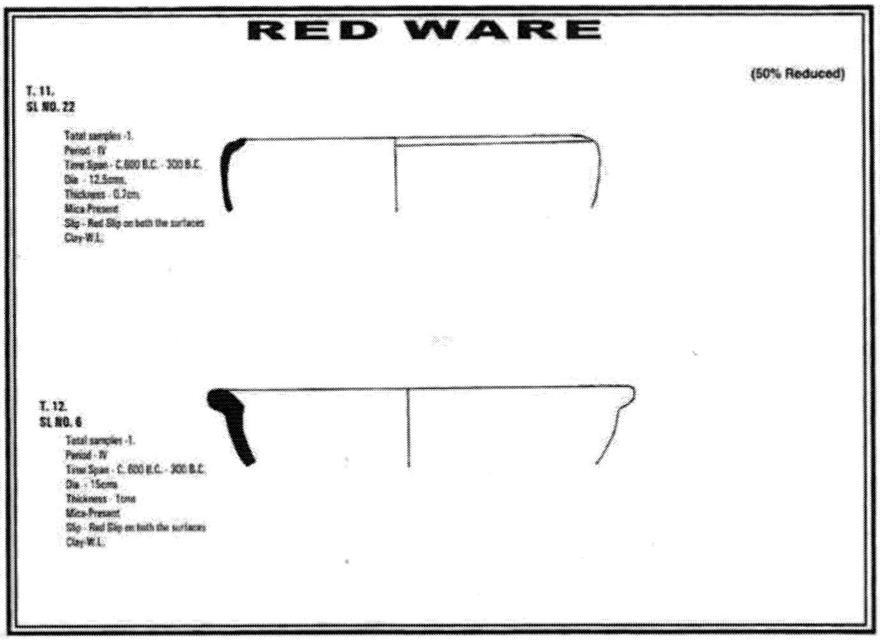

Plate 41

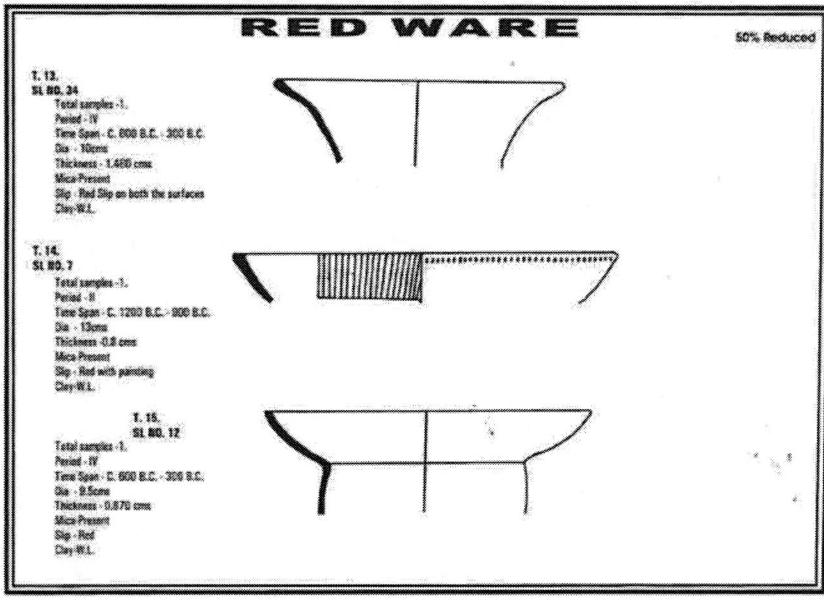

Plate 42

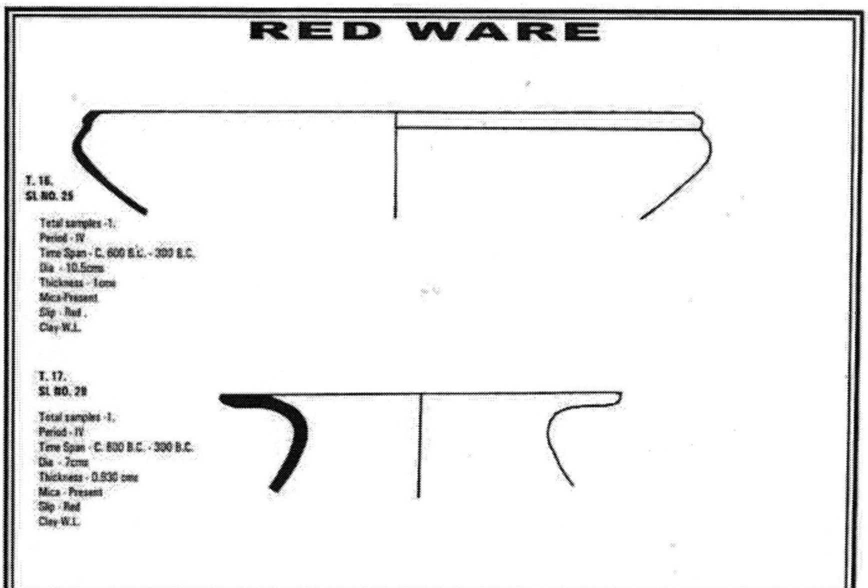

Plate 43

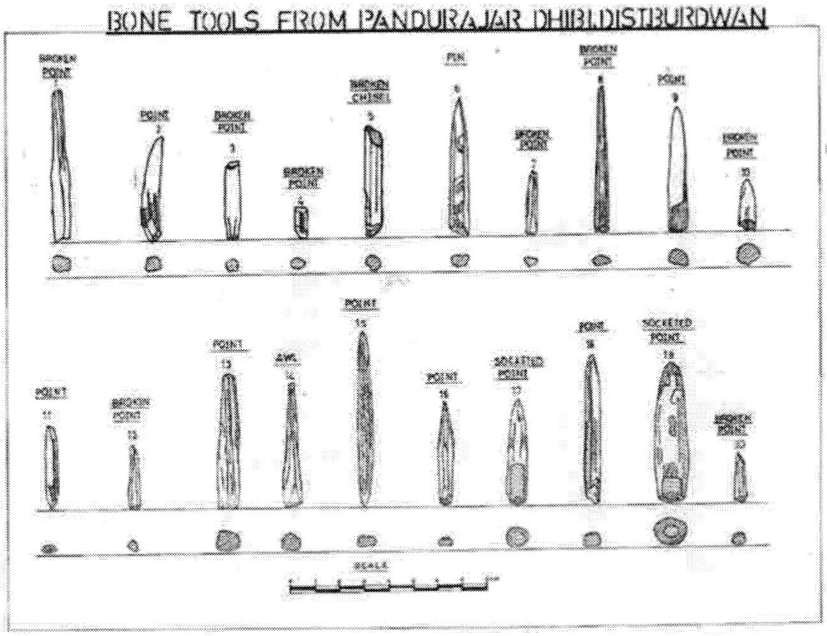

Plate 44

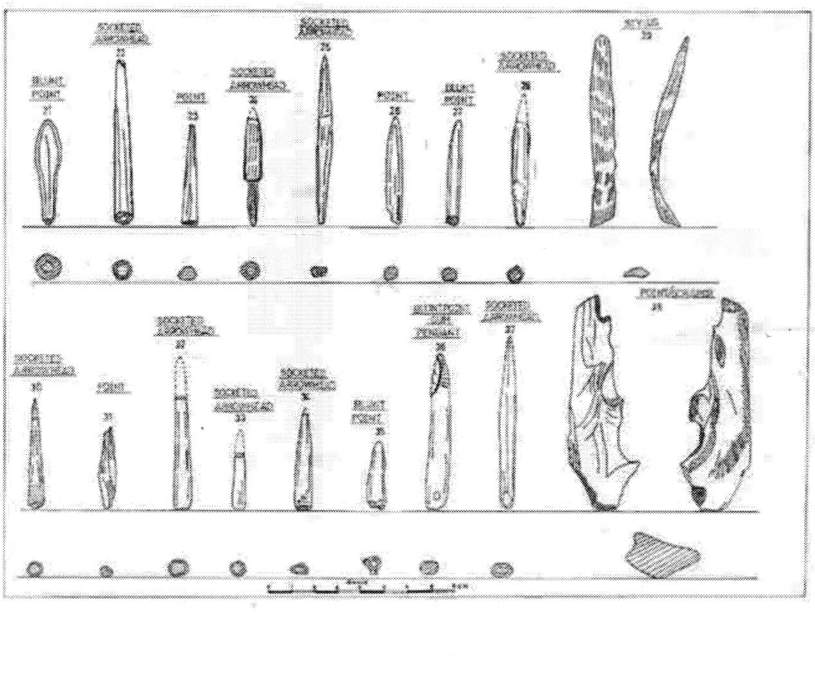

Plate 45

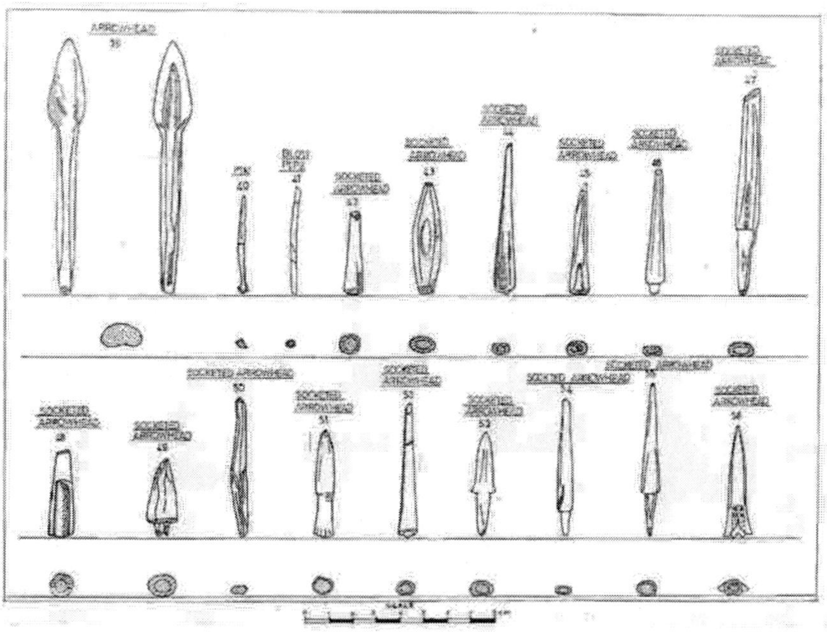

Plate 46

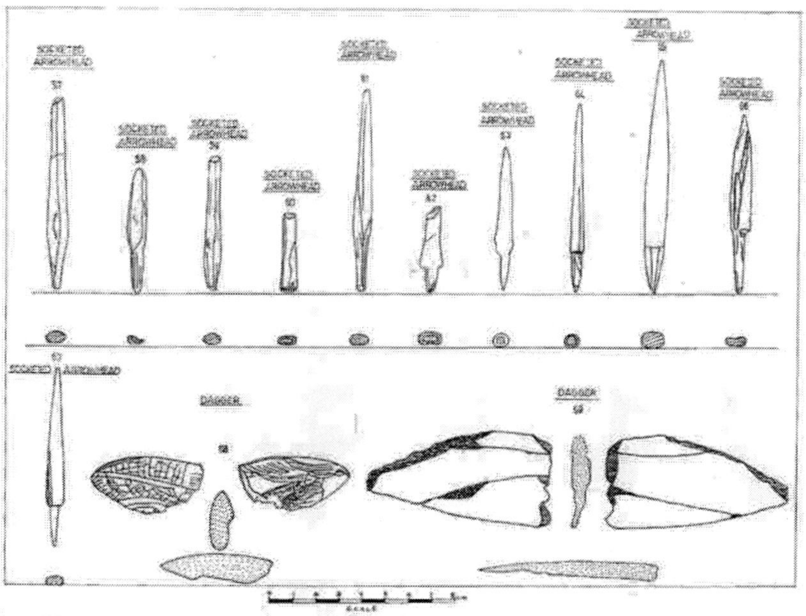

Plate 47

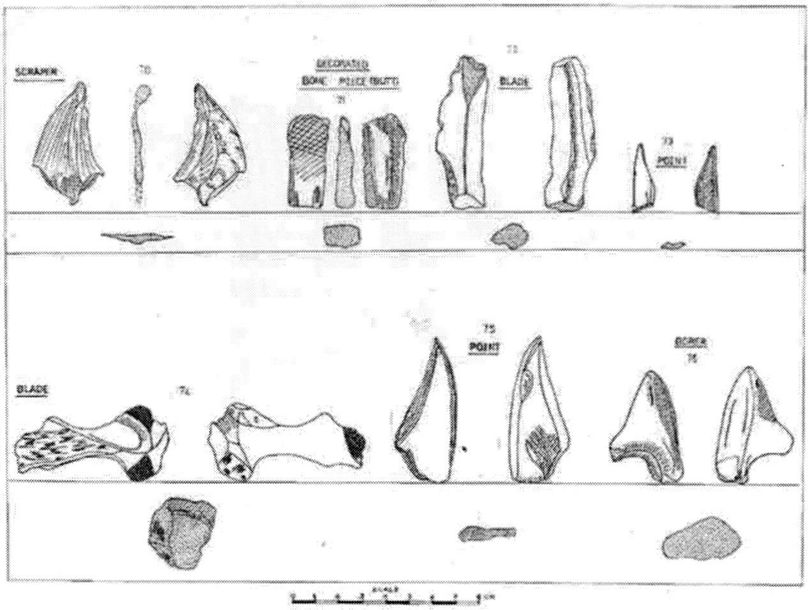

Plate 48

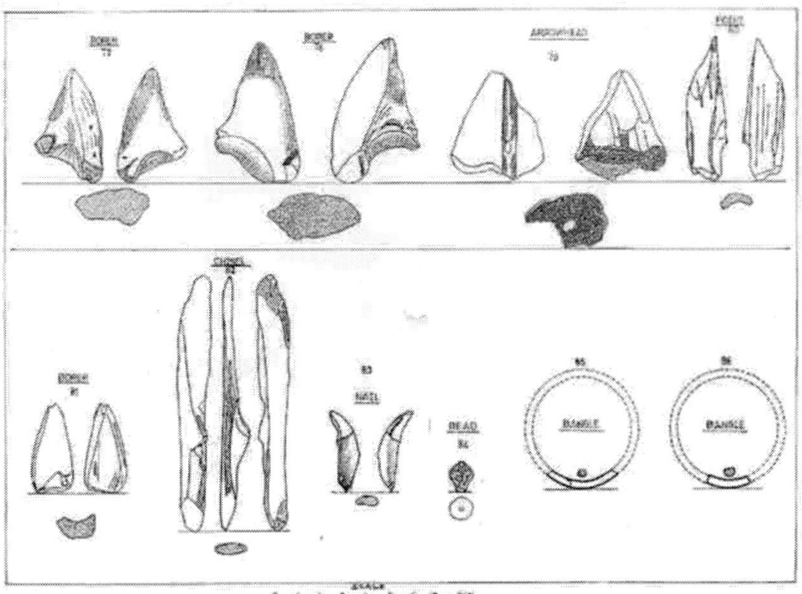

Plate 49

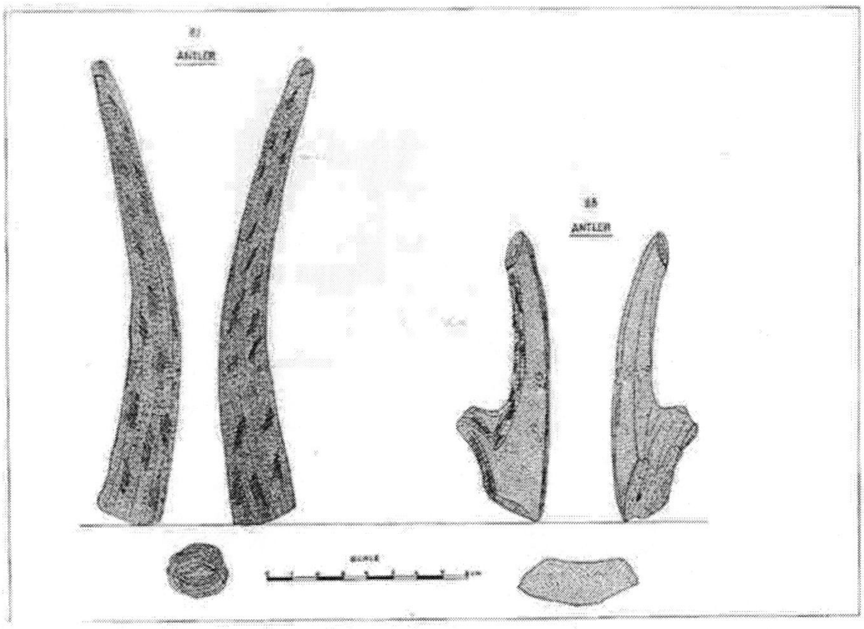

Plate 50

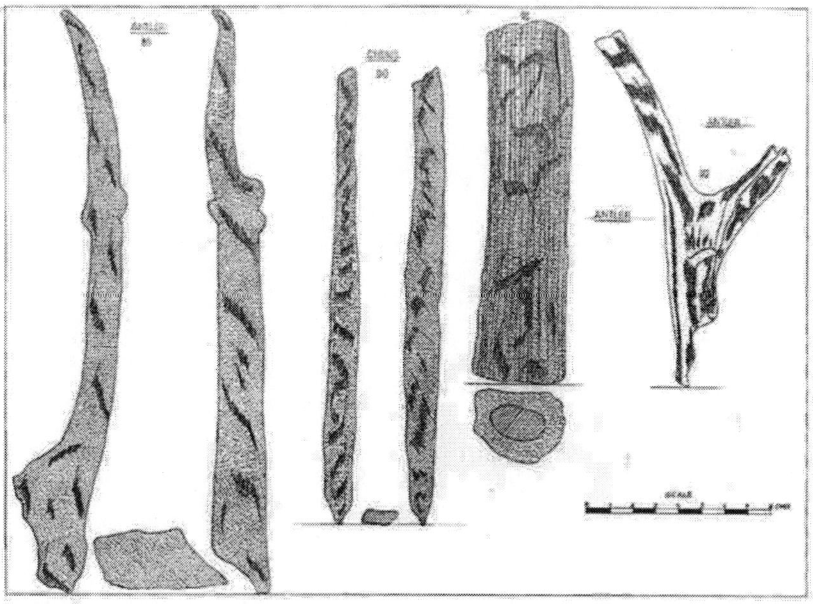

Plate 51

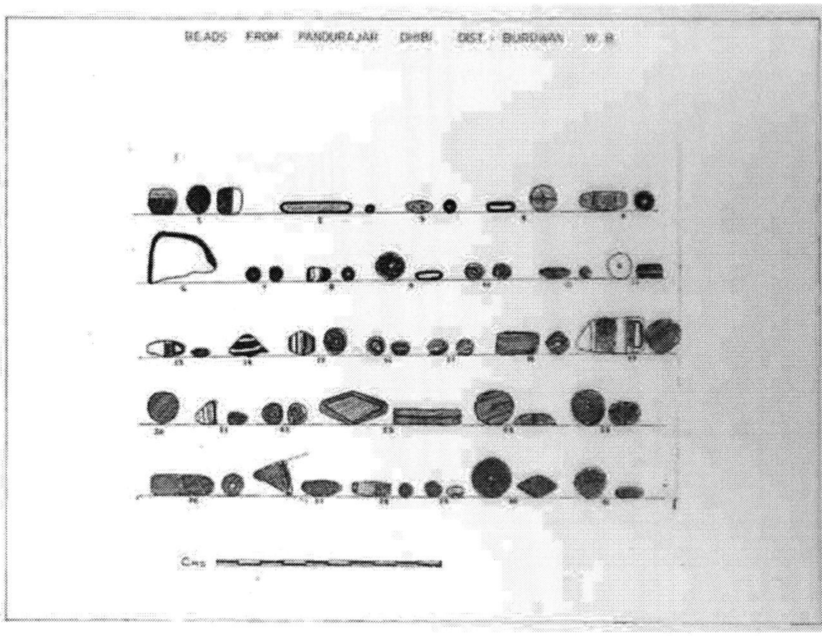

Plate 52

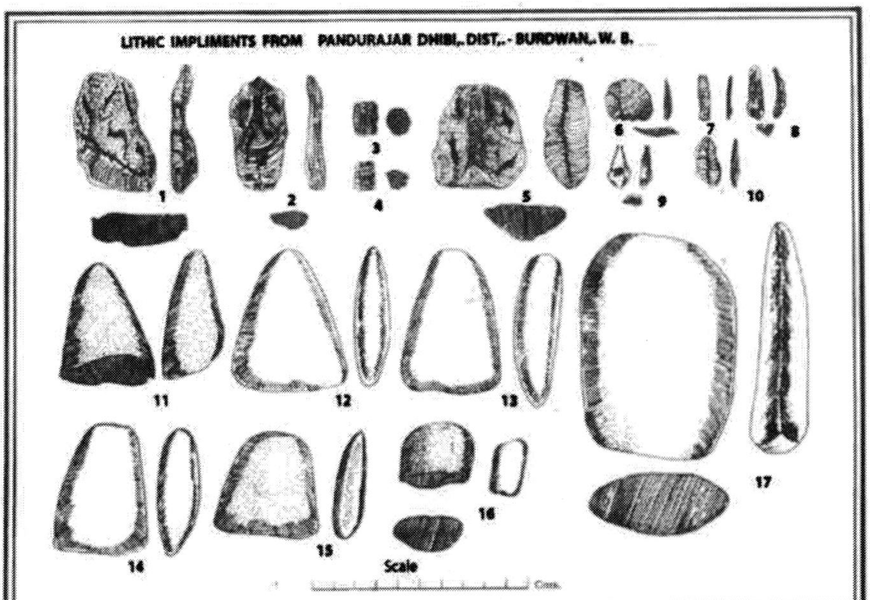

Plate 53

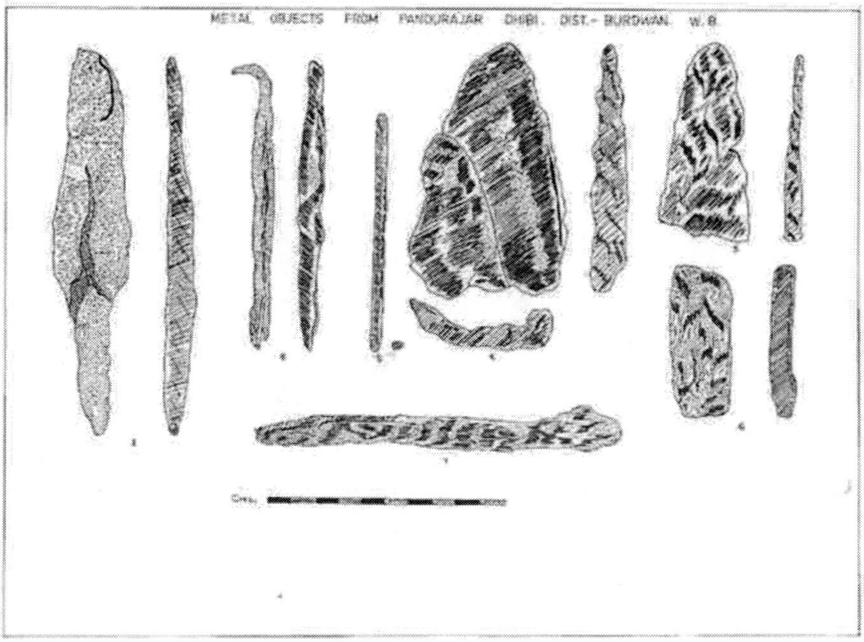

Plate 54

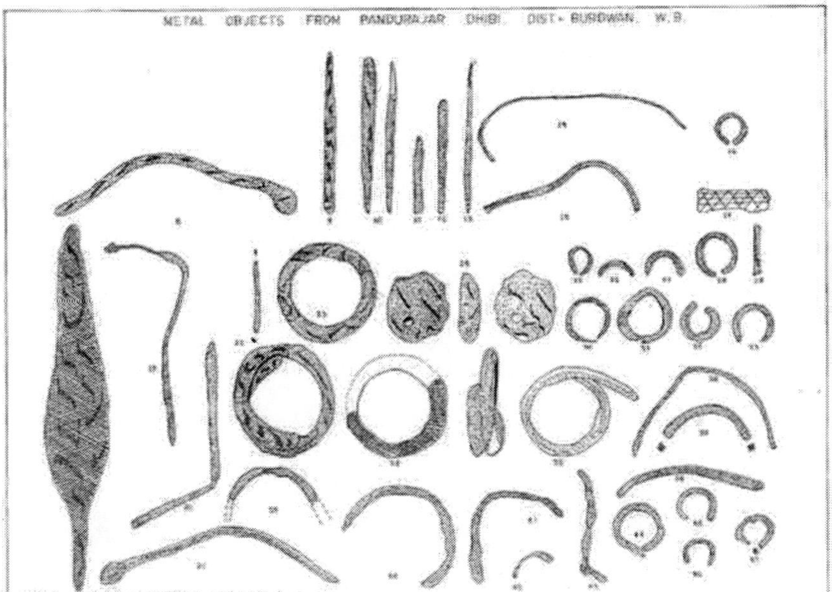

Plate 55

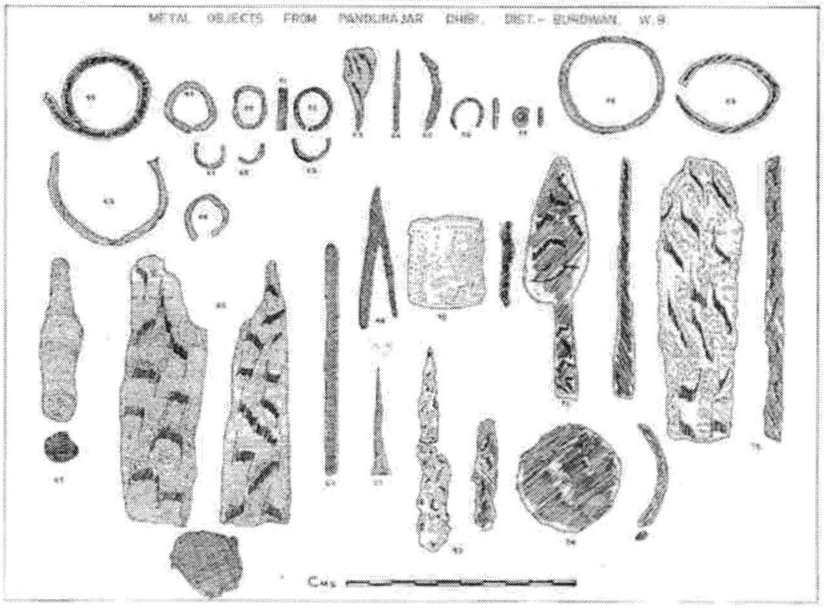

Plate 56

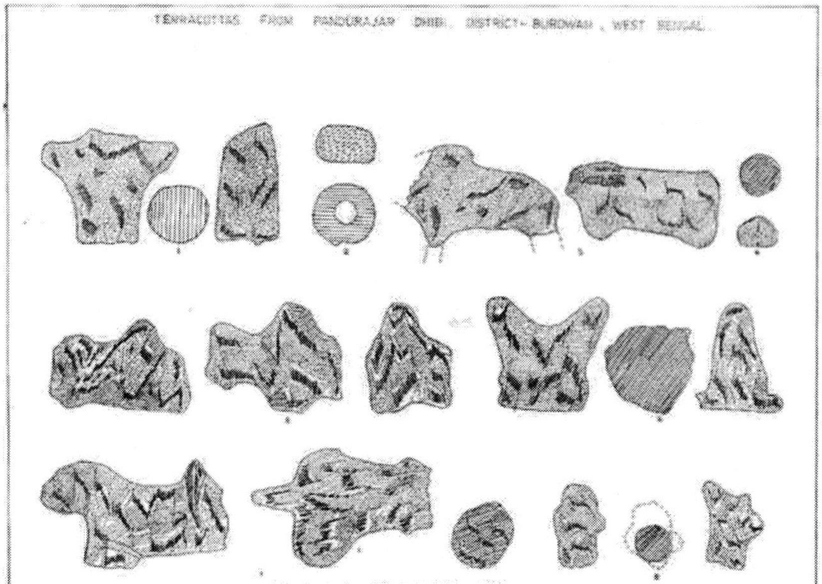

Plate 57

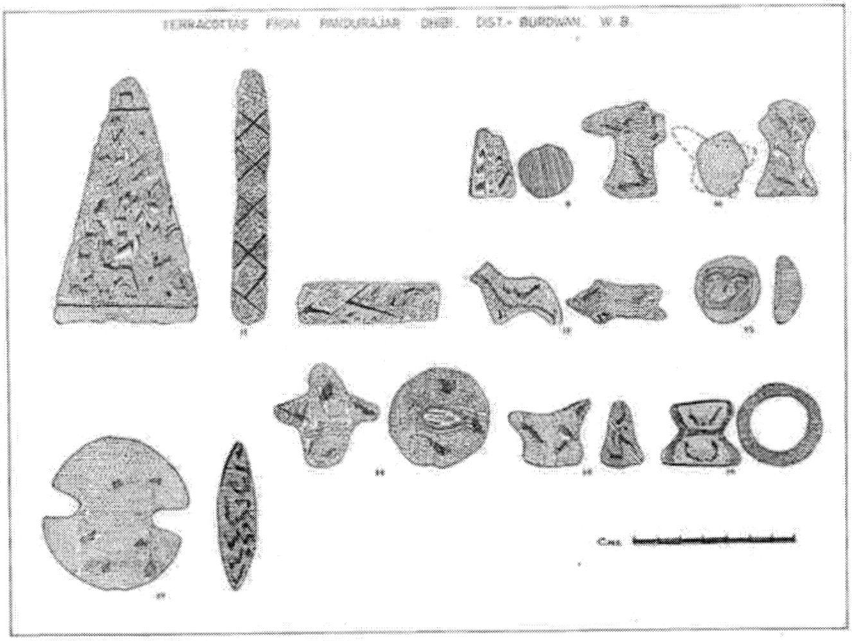

Plate 58

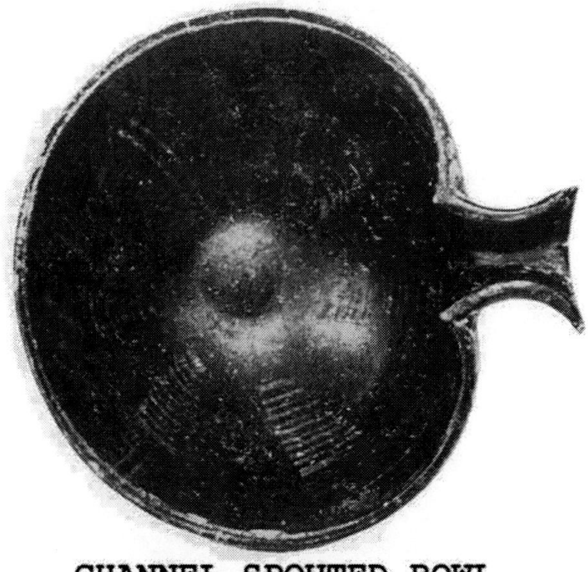

CHANNEL SPOUTED BOWL.
(AFTER DASGUPTA:1964).

Plate 59

Sheet No- 1

BLACK & RED WARE

ITEM NO.- 1 (Bowl for Eating, Drinking & Storage)

TOTAL TYPE :- 9

NUMBER OF SPECIMENTS :- 100

OBSERVATION :- 36.63% OF TOTAL 273 BRW SPECIMENS

TYPE:-	NO:-	PERCENTAGE :-		
V	: 6	= 2.19%	Time Range	--C 1600 B.C. ---300 B.C.
XXIV	: 35	= 12.82%	"	--C 1200 B.C. ---300 B.C.
II	: 8	= 2.83%	"	---C 900 B.C. ---300 B.C.
XII	: 1	= 0.36%	"	---C 900 B.C. ----600 B.C.
XIX	: 3	= 1.09%	"	---C 900 B.C. ----600 B.C.
I	: 23	= 8.42%	"	---C 600 B.C. ----200 AD.
IX	: 5	= 1.83%	"	---C 600 B.C. ----300 B.C.
XXII	: 1	= 0.36%	"	---C 600 B.C. ----300 B.C.
VIII	: 18	= 6.59%	"	---C 600 B.C. ----200 AD.

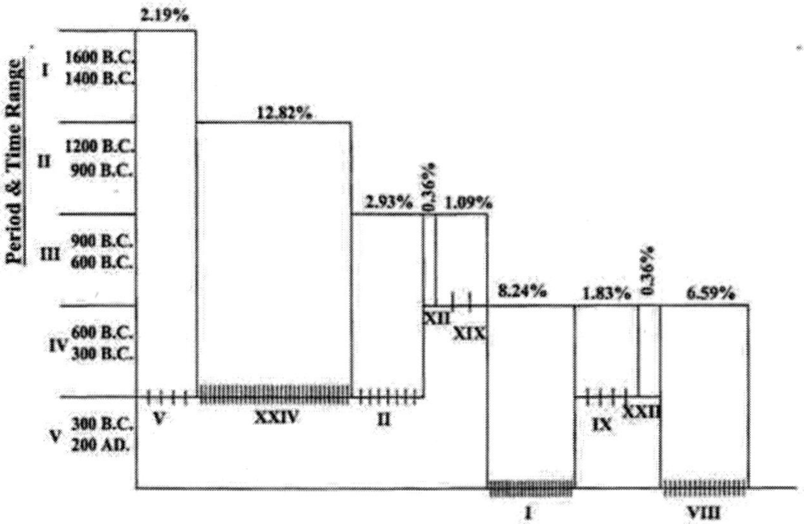

Percentage of occr.with number of occr & type

Plate 60

Sheet No- 2

BLACK & RED WARE

ITEM NO.- 2. (Cooking Vessel/handi)

OBSERVATION :-39.56% OF TOTAL273 BRW SPECIMENS

SL.NO.:-	TYPE:-	NO:-	PERCENTAGE :-	PERIOD /DATE:-
117-208	XXIII	:92	=33.69%	I,II,III,IV C1600 B.C.—300 B.C.
101-105	VI	: 5	= 1.83%	—II,III,IV,V –C 1200 B.C. —200 AD.
106-107	X	:2	= 0.73%	——— III —C 900 B.C. —600 B.C.
108-	XI	:1	= 0.36%	————IV —C 600 B.C. —300 B.C.
109	XII	:1	= 0.36%	———— IV –C 600 B.C. —300 B.C.
110	XIV	:1	= 0.36%	———— IV –C 600 B.C. —300 B.C.
111-112	XVI	:2	= 0.73%	————IV —C 600 B.C. —300 B.C.
113-114	XVIII	:2	= 0.73%	———— IV –C 600 B.C. —300 B.C.
115	XX	:1	= 0.36%	———— IV –C 600 B.C. —300 B.C.
116	XXI	:1	= 0.36%	———— IV –C 600 B.C. —300 B.C.

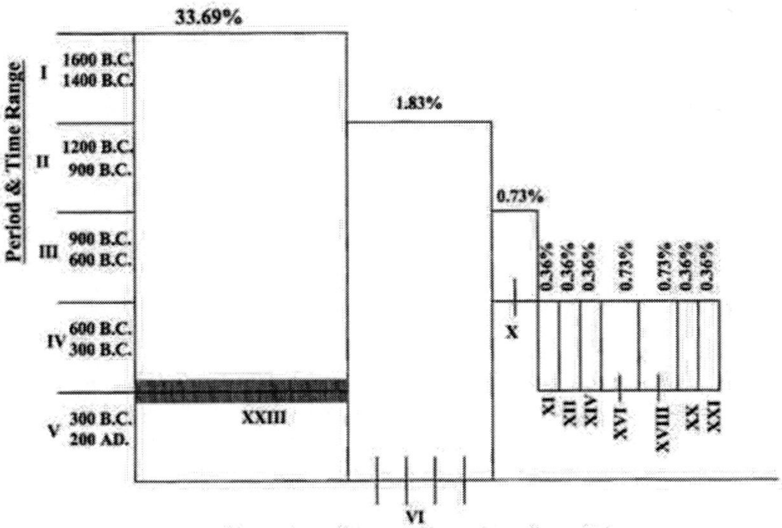

Percentage of occr.with number of occr & type

Plate 61

Sheet No- 3

BLACK & RED WARE

ITEM NO.- 3. Vessel (kalasa)

OBSERVATION :-9.89% OF TOTAL 273 BRW SPECIMENS

SL.NO.:-	TYPE:-	NO:-	PERCENTAGE :-	PERIOD /DATE:-	IDENTIFICATION
216-231	III	:16	= 5.86%	II,III,IV C 1200 B.C. —300 B.C.	KALASA
209-215	III	: 7	=2.56%	———IV –C 600 B.C. —300 B.C.	KALASA
232-235	VII	:4	= 1.46%	———IV—C 600 B.C. —300 B.C.	KALASA

ITEM NO.- 4. goblet (khupo)

OBSERVATION :- 0.36% OF TOTAL 273 BRW SPECIMENS

SL.NO.:-	TYPE:-	NO:-	PERCENTAGE :-	PERIOD /DATE:-	IDENTIFICATION
236	XV	:1	= 0.36%	————IV —C 600 B.C. —300 B.C.	KHUPO

ITEM NO.- 5. funnel (kupi)

OBSERVATION :- 0.73% OF TOTAL 273 BRW SPECIMENS

SL.NO.:-	TYPE:-	NO:-	PERCENTAGE :-	PERIOD /DATE:-	IDENTIFICATION
237-238	XVII	:2	= 0.73%	————III —C 900 B.C. —600 B.C.	KHUPI

ITEM NO.- 6. Channel Spouted Bowl

OBSERVATION :- 12.82% OF TOTAL 273 BRW SPECIMENS

SL.NO.:-	TYPE:-	NO:-	PERCENTAGE :-	PERIOD /DATE:-	IDENTIFICATION
238-273	XXV	:35	= 12.82%	—II III IV C 1200B.C.—300B.C.	OFFERING BOWL/ DRINKING GOBLET

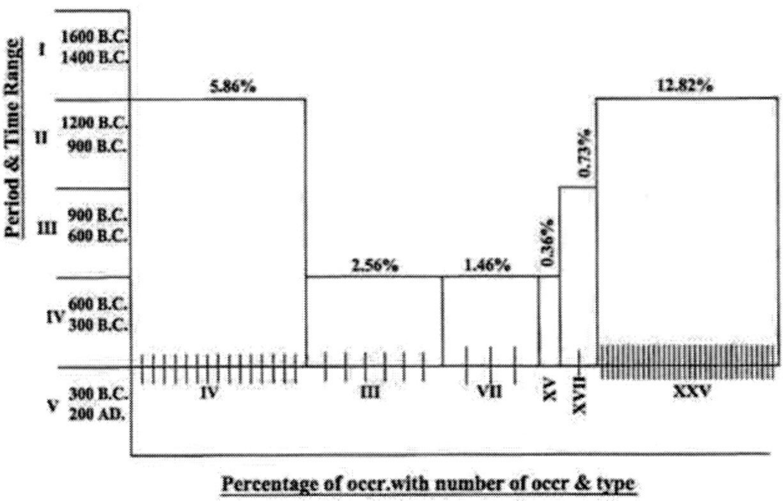

Percentage of occr.with number of occr & type

Plate 62

Sheet No- 4

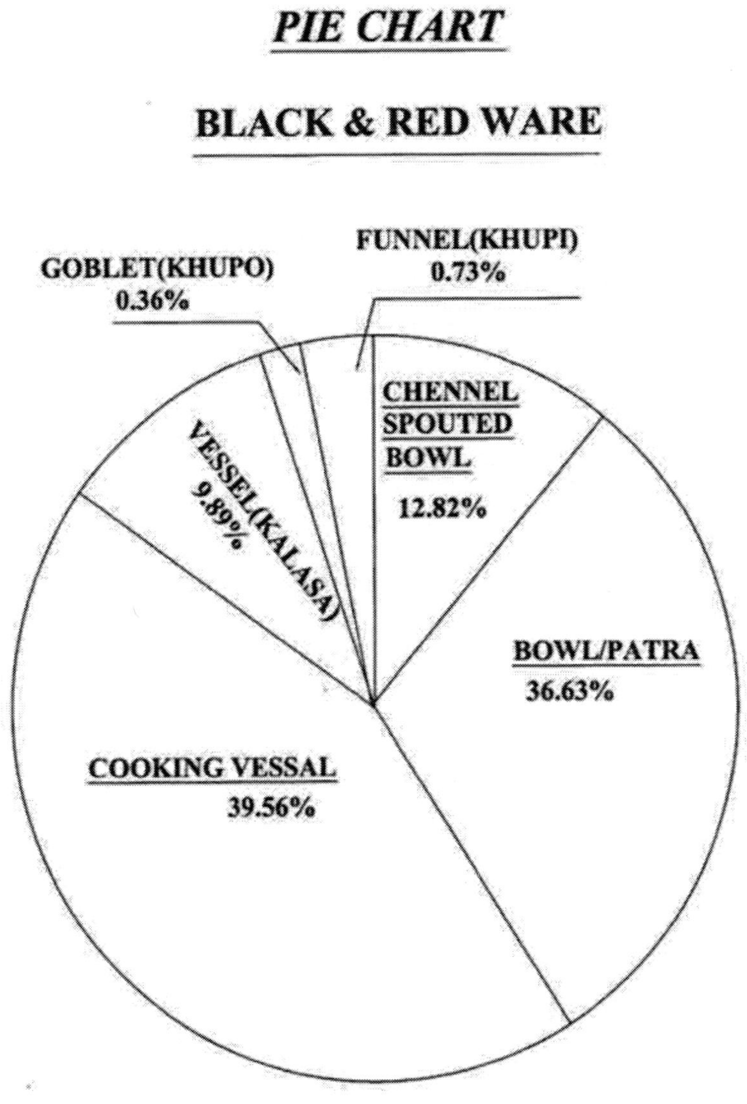

Plate 63

Sheet No- 5

BLACK WARE

ITEM NO.- 1. dish (patra)

OBSERVATION :- 26.29% OF TOTAL 133 BW SPECIMENS

SL.NO.:-	TYPE:-	NO:-	PERCENTAGE :-	PERIOD /DATE:-	IDENTIFICATION:-
27-31	IV	: 5	= 3.75%	I, IV — C 1600 B.C. —1400 B.C. C 600 B.C. —300 B.C.	PATRA
1-26	IV	: 26	= 19.54%	IV —C 600 B.C. —300 B.C.	PATRA
32-33	IX	:2	= 1.50%	IV —C 600 B.C. —300 B.C.	PATRA
34-35	XIX	:2	= 1.50%	IV —C 600 B.C. —300 B.C.	PATRA

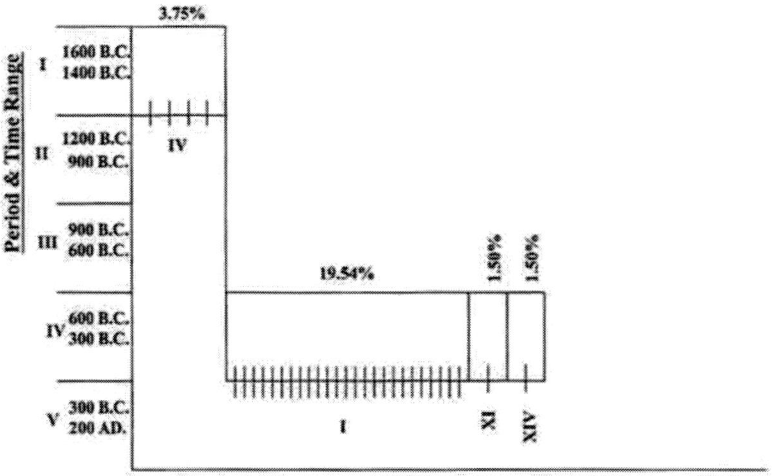

Percentage of occr.with number of occr & type

Plate 64

Sheet No- 6

BLACK WARE

ITEM NO.- 2. (patra)

OBSERVATION :- 32.28% OF TOTAL 133 BW SPECIMENS

SL.NO.:-	TYPE:-	NO:-	PERCENTAGE :-	PERIOD /DATE:-	IDENTIFICATION:-
77-78	XVI	: 2	= 1.50%	----II,IV-----C 1200 B.C. ---900 B.C. C 600 B.C. ---300 B.C.	PATRA
36-42	XXVIII	:7	= 5.26%	-------- III,IV ---C 900 B.C. ---300 B.C.	PATRA
43-51	II	:9	= 6.76%	-----------IV ---C 600 B.C. ---300 B.C.	PATRA
52-55	III	:4	= 3.00%	----------- IV --C 600 B.C. ---300 B.C.	PATRA
56-64	V	:9	= 6.76%	----------- IV --C 600 B.C. ---300 B.C.	PATRA
65-67	VIII	:3	= 2.25%	-----------IV ---C 600 B.C. ---300 B.C.	PATRA
68-69	XII	:2	= 1.50%	----------- V --C 600 B.C. ---300 B.C.	PATRA
70-71	XV	:2	= 1.50%	----------- IV --C 600 B.C. ---300 B.C.	PATRA
72	XXII	:1	= 0.75%	----------- IV --C 600 B.C. ---300 B.C.	PATRA
73	XXIII	:1	= 0.75%	----------- IV --C 600 B.C. ---300 B.C.	PATRA
74	XXV	:1	= 0.75%	----------- IV --C 600 B.C. ---300 B.C.	PATRA
75	XXVI	:1	= 0.75%	----------- IV --C 600 B.C. ---300 B.C.	PATRA
76	XXVII	:1	= 0.75%	----------- IV --C 600 B.C. ---300 B.C.	PATRA

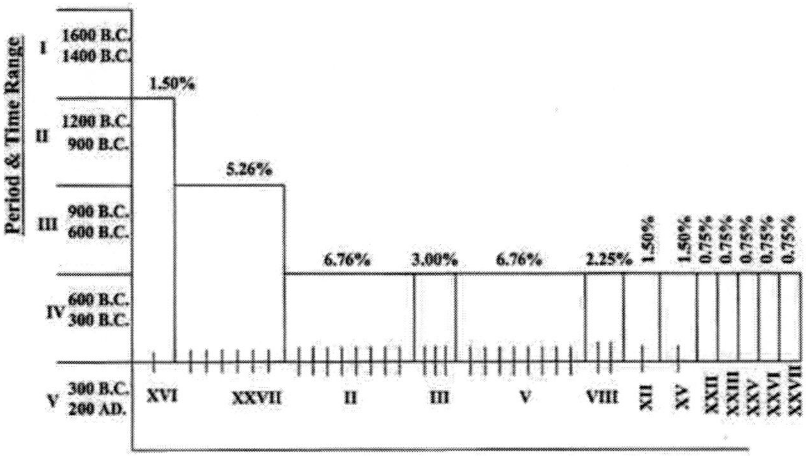

VI

Percentage of occr.with number of occr & type

Plate 65

Sheet No- 7

BLACK WARE

ITEM NO.- 3. cooking vessel(handi)

OBSERVATION :- 12 % OF TOTAL 133 BRW SPECIMENS

SL.NO.:-	TYPE:-	NO:-	PERCENTAGE :-	PERIOD /DATE:-	IDENTIFICATION
84-86	X	:3	= 2.25% -----	III,IV---- C 900 B.C. ---300 B.C.	HANDI
79-83	VI	: 5	= 3.75% ---------	IV----- --C 600 B.C. -------300 B.C.	HANDI
87-88	XIII	: 2	= 1.50% ---------	IV----- --C 600 B.C. -------300 B.C.	HANDI
89-90	XVII	: 2	= 1.50% ---------	IV----- --C 600 B.C. -------300 B.C.	HANDI
91-92	XVIII	: 2	= 1.50% ---------	IV----- --C 600 B.C. -------300 B.C.	HANDI
93-94	XIX	: 2	= 1.50% ---------	IV----- --C 600 B.C. -------300 B.C.	HANDI

ITEM NO.- 9. Channel Spouted Bowl

OBSERVATION :- 21.05% OF TOTAL 133 BW SPECIMENS

SL.NO.:-	TYPE:-	NO:-	PERCENTAGE :-	PERIOD /DATE:-	IDENTIFICATION
104-131	XI	:28	=21.05%---------	III----IV--C 900B.C.---600B.C.	Drinking pot/ offering bowl

ITEM NO.- 10 Dish on stand

OBSERVATION :- 1.50% OF TOTAL 133 BW SPECIMENS

SL.NO.:-	TYPE:-	NO:-	PERCENTAGE :-	PERIOD /DATE:-	IDENTIFICATION
132-133	XI	:2	= 1.50% -------------	IV ---C 600 B.C. ----300 B.C.	Eating food artical

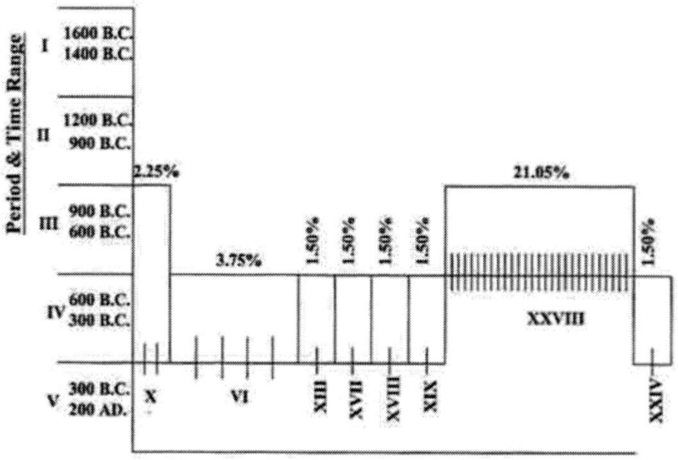

Percentage of occr.with number of occr & type

Plate 66

Sheet No- 8

BLACK WARE

ITEM NO.- 4. fry-pan (kada)

OBSERVATION :- 3.0 % OF TOTAL 133 BW SPECIMENS

SL.NO.:-	TYPE:-	NO:-	PERCENTAGE :-	PERIOD /DATE:-	IDENTIFICATION
95-98	VII	:4	=3.00%————V————	C 600B.C.——300 B.C.	KADA

ITEM NO.- 5. vessel (kalasa)

OBSERVATION :- 1.50% OF TOTAL 133 BW SPECIMENS

SL.NO.:-	TYPE:-	NO:-	PERCENTAGE :-	PERIOD /DATE:-	IDENTIFICATION
99-100	XI	:2	= 1.50% ————IV	—C 600 B.C. —-300 B.C.	Kkalasa

ITEM NO.- 6. flower vase (phul dani)

OBSERVATION :- 0.75% OF TOTAL 133 BW SPECIMENS

SL.NO.:-	TYPE:-	NO:-	PERCENTAGE :-	PERIOD /DATE:-	IDENTIFICATION
101	XX	:1	= 0.75% ————III	—C 900 B.C. —600 B.C.	DECORATION

ITEM NO.- 7. basin (gamta)

OBSERVATION :- 0.757% OF TOTAL 133 BW SPECIMENS

SL.NO.:-	TYPE:-	NO:-	PERCENTAGE :-	PERIOD /DATE:-	IDENTIFICATION
102	XXI	:1	= 0.75% ————IV	—C 600 B.C. —300 B.C.	GRAINS STARING OF FOOD

ITEM NO.- 8. trough (jabna- bhanda)

OBSERVATION :- 0.75% OF TOTAL 133 BW SPECIMENS

SL.NO.:-	TYPE:-	NO:-	PERCENTAGE :-	PERIOD /DATE:-	IDENTIFICATION
103	XXIV	:1	= 0.75% ————IV	—C 600 B.C. —300 B.C.	GRAINS STARING OF FOOD

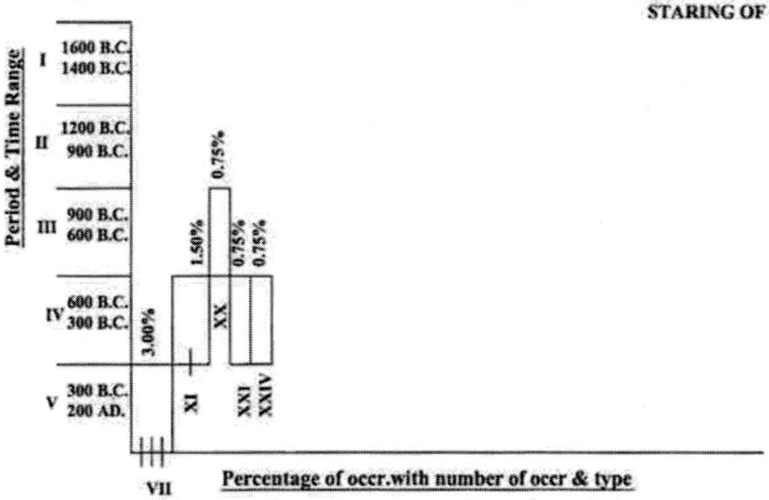

Plate 67

Sheet No- 9

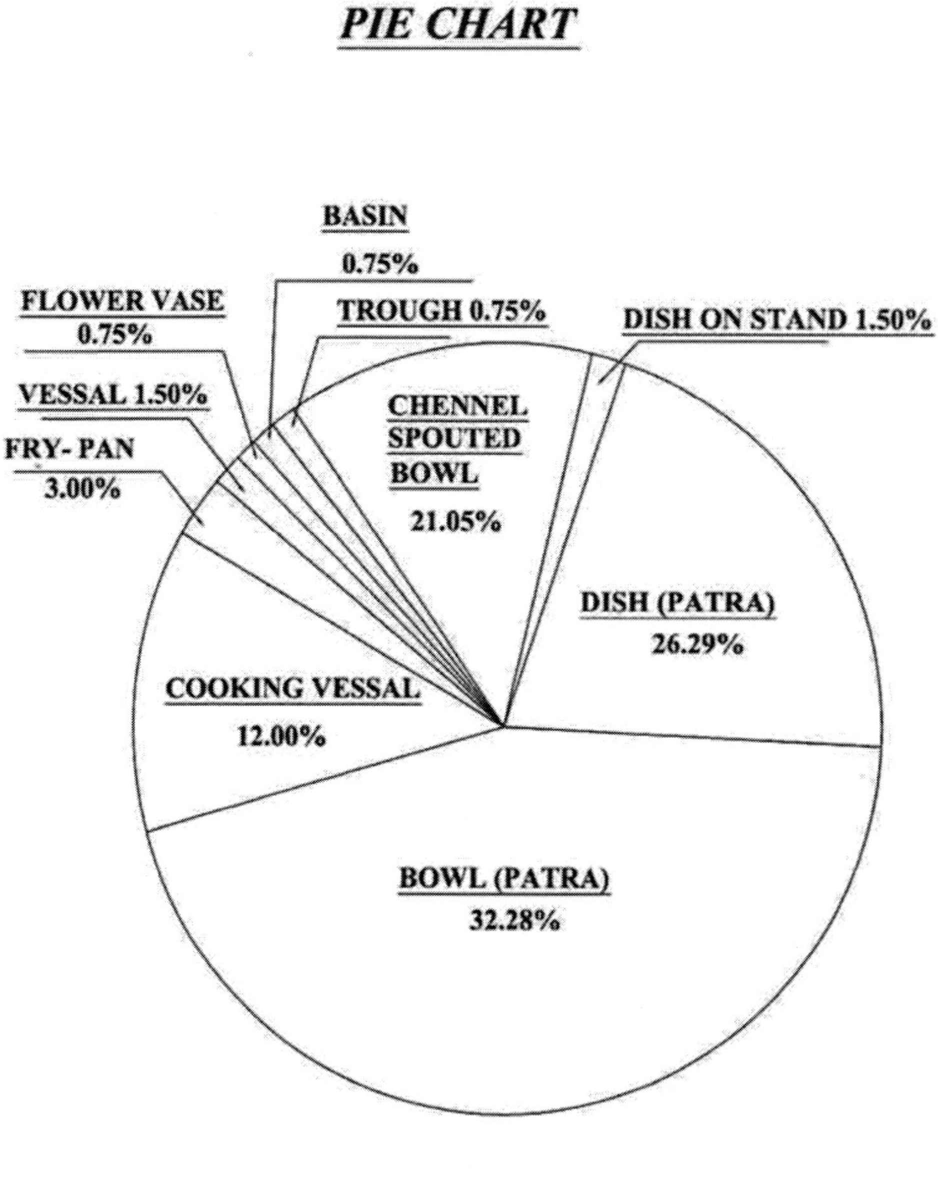

Plate 68

Sheet No- 10

RED WARE

ITEM NO.- Kitchen utensil

OBSERVATION :- TOTAL 38 RW SPECIMENS

SL.NO.:-	TYPE:-	NO:-	PERCENTAGE :-	PERIOD /DATE:-	IDENTIFICATION:-
1-13	I,II,VIII,X	: 13	= 34.21%	----II,III,IV------C 1200 B.C. ----300 B.C.	HANDI
21-27	IV,XI,XIV,XVI	:7	= 18.42%	--------- II,IV ---C 1200 B.C. ----900 B.C. C 600 B.C. —300 B.C.	BOWL
28-29	III,IV	:2	= 5.26%	-------------III,IV ---C 900 B.C. ----300 B.C.	VESSEL
14-20	III,IV,XII	:7	= 18.42%	------------- IV,V --C 600 B.C. ---200 AD.	BASIN
30-31	IV	:2	= 5.26%	------------ IV --C 600 B.C. ----300 B.C.	DISH
32	XIII	:2	= 5.26%	------------IV ---C 600 B.C. ----300 B.C.	FUNNEL SHAPED POT
33	XV	:1	=2.63%	-------------IV--C 600 B.C.------300 B.C.	JUICE/WINE CONTAINER
34	XVII	:1	= 2.63%	------------ IV --C 600 B.C. ----300 B.C.	GHATA
35-36	XVIII	:2	= 5.26%	----------------IV--C 600 B.C.-----300 B.C.	CHANNEL SPOUTED BOWL

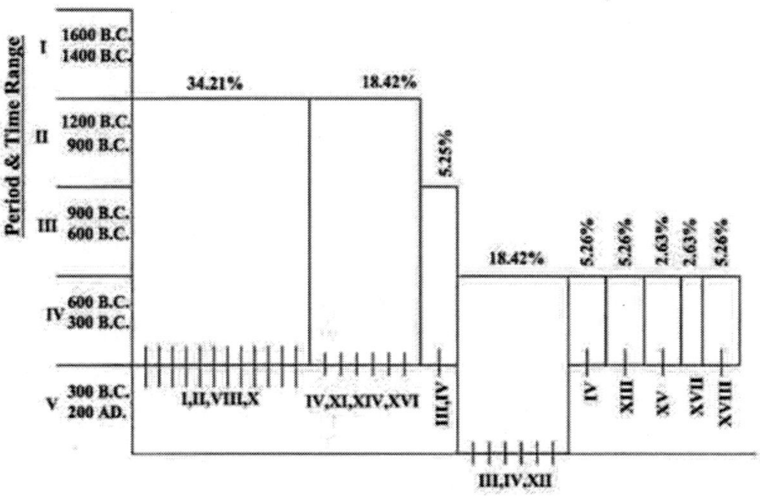

Percentage of occr.with number of occr & type

Plate 69

Sheet No- 11

PIE CHART

KITCHEN UTENSIL (RED WARE)

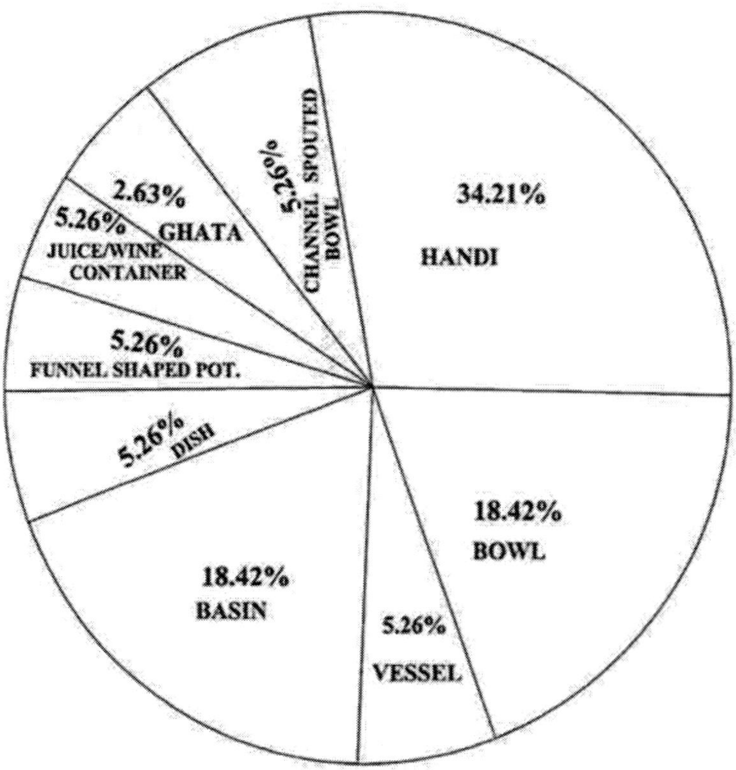

Plate 70

Sheet No- 12

Bone & Antler : Arranged Period wise

OBSERVATION :- 14.14% OF TOTAL 92 BONE ANTLER SPECIMENS

SL.NO.:-	TYPE:-	NO:-	PERCENTAGE :-	PERIOD /DATE:-	INEDTIFICATION
1-8	POINT	:8	= 8.70%	I — C 1600 B.C. —1400 B.C.	PIERCING/HUNTING TOOL
9-10	ANTLER	: 2	= 2.17%	IV —C 1600 B.C. —1400 B.C.	CORE
11	SOCKETED ARROW HEAD	:1	=1.09%	I—C1600 B.C.—1400 B.C.	HUNTING TOOL
12	BLAND	:1	=1.09%	I—C1600 B.C.—1400 B.C.	CUTTING TOOL
13	BEAD	:1	=1.09%	I—C1600 B.C.—1400 B.C.	ORNAMENTS

OBSERVATION :- 10.87% OF TOTAL 92 BONE & ANTLER SPECIMENS

SL.NO.:-	TYPE:-	NO:-	PERCENTAGE :-	PERIOD /DATE:-	IDENTIFICATION
14–19	POINT	:6	= 6.52%	III —C 1200 B.C. —900 B.C.	PIERCING/HUNTING
20-23	SOCKTED ARROW HEAD	:4	= 4.35%	III —C 1200 B.C. —900 B.C.	PIERCING/HUNTING

OBSERVATION :- 7.60% OF TOTAL 92BONE & ANTLER SPECIMENS

SL.NO.:-	TYPE:-	NO:-	PERCENTAGE :-	PERIOD /DATE:-	INDENTIFICATION
24-25	POINT	:2	= 2.17%	III —C 900 B.C. —600 B.C.	HUNTING/PIERCING TOOL
26-30	SOCKTED ARROW HEAD	:5	= 5.43%	III —C 900 B.C. —600 B.C.	PIERCING/HUNTING TOOL

Plate 71

Sheet No-13

OBSERVATION :- 65.23% OF TOTAL 92 BONE ANTLER SPECIMENS

SL.NO.:-	TYPE:-	NO:-	PERCENTAGE :-	PERIOD /DATE:-	IDENTIFICATION
31-55	SOCKETED ARROW HEAD	:25	= 27.17%	IV — C 600 B.C. —300 B.C.	HUNTING TOOL
56-67	POINT	:12	= 13.04%	IV —C 600 B.C. —300 B.C.	HUNTING TOOL
68–71	BORER	:4	= 4.35%	IV —C 600 B.C. —300 B.C.	HUNTING TOOL
72–75	ANTLER	:4	= 4.35%	IV —C 600 B.C. —300 B.C.	CORE
76–77	ARROW HEAD	:2	= 2.17%	IV —C 600 B.C. —300 B.C.	HUNTING TOOL
78–79	DAGGER	:2	= 2.17%	IV —C 600 B.C. —300 B.C.	HUNTING TOOL
80–81	CHISEL	:2	= 2.17%	IV —C 600 B.C. —300 B.C.	DIGGING TOOL
82	AWL	:1	= 1.09%	IV —C 600 B.C. —300 B.C.	FOR PERFORATION
83	STYLUS	:1	= 1.09%	IV —C 600 B.C. —300 B.C.	ORNAMENTS ONE SELF
84	PIN	:1	= 1.09%	IV —C 600 B.C. —300 B.C.	PERFORATION
85	BLOW PIPE	:1	= 1.09%	IV —C 600 B.C. —300 B.C.	GOLDSMITH
86	SCRAPER	:1	= 1.09%	IV —C 600 B.C. —300 B.C.	SCRAPING
87	NAIL	:1	= 1.09%	IV —C 600 B.C. —300 B.C.	PIERCING
88	BLADE	:1	= 1.09%	IV —C 600 B.C. —300 B.C.	CUTTING
89	BANGLE	:1	= 1.09%	IV —C 600 B.C. —300 B.C.	ORNAMENT
90	DECORATED BONE PIPE	:1	= 1.09%	IV —C 600 B.C. —300 B.C.	ORNAMENTS

OBSERVATION :- 2.17% OF TOTAL 238 BONE & ANTLER SPECIMENS

SL.NO.:-	TYPE:-	NO:-	PERCENTAGE :-	PERIOD /DATE:-	IDENTIFICATION
91-92	POINT	:2	= 2.17%	V —C 300 B.C. —200 AD.	HUNTING TOOL

Plate 72

Sheet No- 14

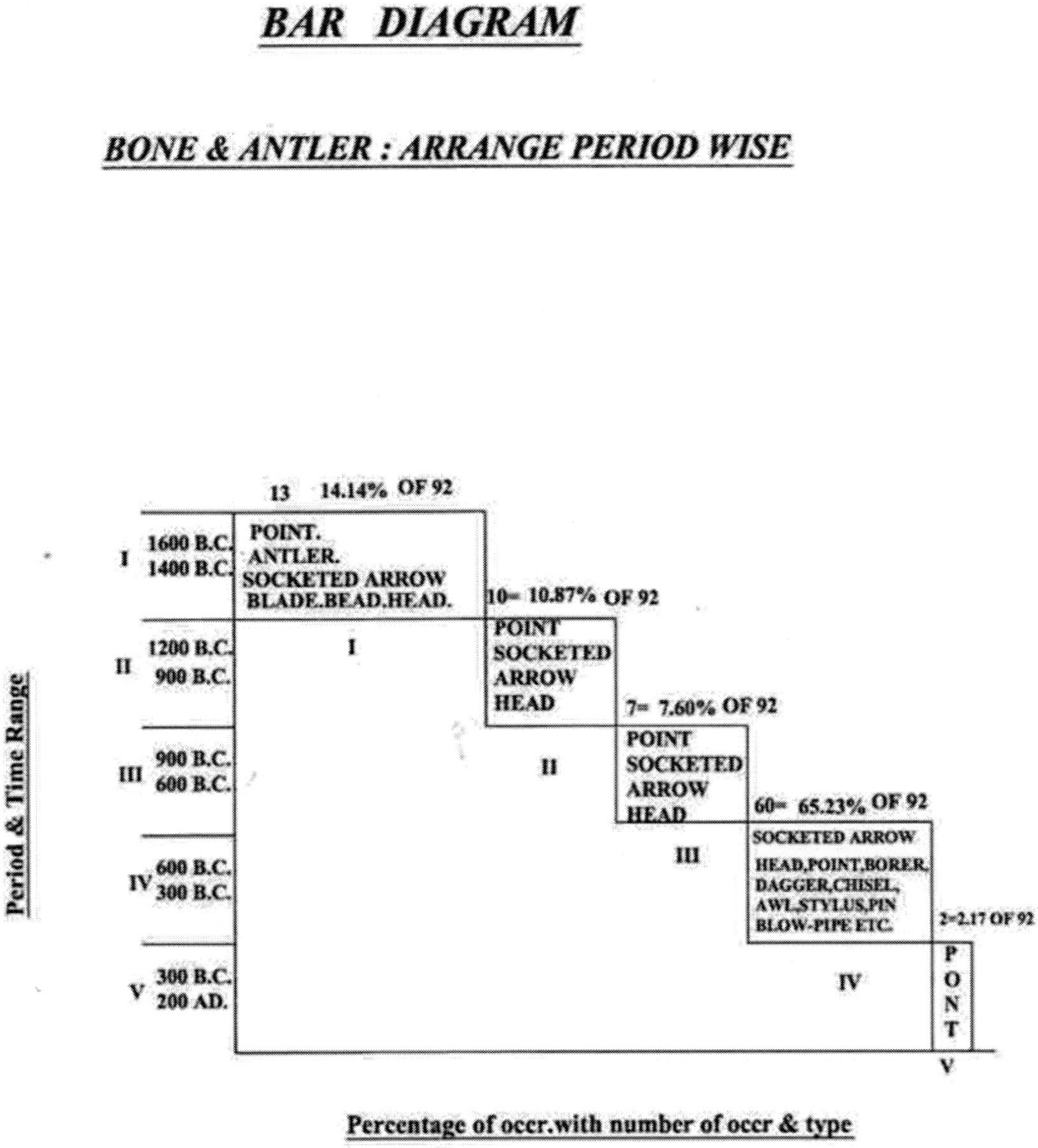

Plate 73

Sheet No- 15

PIE CHART

BONE & ANTLER : ARRANGE PERIOD WISE

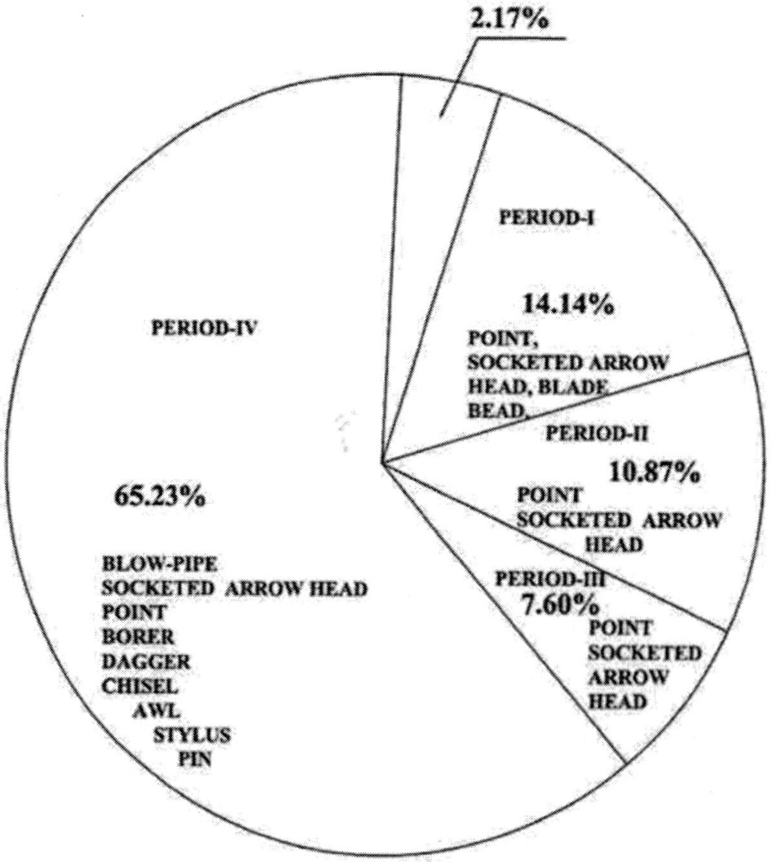

Plate 74

Sheet No- 16

Metal object : Arranged Period wise

Number Of Specimens- 74

Copper - 59
Iron- 15

OBSERVATION :- 10.81% OF TOTAL 74 METAL OBJECTS (COPPER)

SL.NO.:-	TYPE:-	NO:-	PESENTAGE:-	PERIOD /DATE:-	IDENTIFICATION
1-6	COPPER STYLUS	:6	= 8.11%	II C 1200 B.C. —1900 B.C.	USED FOR ORNAMENTATION
7	COPPER BANGLE	:1	= 1.35%	——II–C 1200 B.C. —900 B.C.	ORNAMENTATION
8	COPPER SPEAR HEAD	:1	= 1.35%	——II–C 1200 B.C. —900 B.C.	HUNTING

OBSERVATION :- 12.16% OF TOTAL 74 METAL OBJECT(COPPER)

SL.NO.:-	TYPE:-	NO:-	PESENTAGE:-	PERIOD /DATE:-	IDENTIFICATION
9	WIRE	:1	= 1.35%	————III —C 900 B.C. —600 B.C.	USED FOR HANGING
10-13	BANGLE	:4	= 5.41%	————III —C 900 B.C. —600 B.C.	ORNAMENT
14	RING	:1	= 1.35%	————III —C 900 B.C. —600 B.C.	ORNAMENT
15	STYLUS	:1	= 1.35%	————III—C 900B.C.—600 B.C.	USED FOR ORNAMENTATION
16	PIN	:1	= 1.35%	————III —C 900 B.C. —600 B.C.	USED FOR FIXING MINOR OBJECT
17	ORE	:1	= 1.35%	————III —C 900 B.C. —600 B.C.	USED FOR CORE

OBSERVATION :- 18.92% OF TOTAL 74 METAL OBJECT(COPPER)

SL.NO.:-	TYPE:-	NO:-	PESENTAGE:-	PERIOD /DATE:-	IDENTIFICATION
18	STYLUS	:1	=1.35%	————IV—C 600 B.C.—300B.C.	USED FOR ORNAMENTATION
19-26	RING	:8	=10.81%	————IV—C 600 B.C.—300 B.C.	USED AS ORNAMENT
27	PIN	:1	= 1.35%	————IV —C 600 B.C. —300 B.C.	USED FOR FIXING
28-31	BANGLE	:4	= 5.41%	————IV —C 600 B.C. —300 B.C.	ORNAMENT

Plate 75

Sheet No- 17

Metal object : Arranged Period wise

Number Of Specimens- 74

Copper - 59
iron- 15

OBSERVATION :- 37.83% OF TOTAL 74 METAL OBJECT(COPPER)

SL.NO.:-	TYPE:-	NO:-	PESENTAGE:-	PERIOD /DATE:-	IDENTIFICATION
32-44	COPPER RING	:13	= 17.57%	V —C 300 B.C. —200 AD.	ORNAMENTS
45-51	BANGLE	:7	= 9.46%	V —C 300 B.C. —200 AD.	ORNAMENT
52-54	STYLUS	:3	= 4.05%	V —C 300 B.C. —200 AD.	USED FOR ORNAMENTATION
55-56	SPIRAL WIRE	:2	= 2.70%	V —C 300 B.C. —200 AD.	USED FOR HANGING
57	PLATE	:1	= 1.35%	V —C 300 B.C. —200 AD.	PORTION OF CONTAINER
58	SPOON	:1	= 1.35%	V —C 300 B.C. —200 AD.	KITCHEN UTENSIL
59	PIN	:1	= 1.35%	V —C 300 B.C. —200 AD.	FOR FIXING MIRROR OBCT.

OBSERVATION :- 2.70% OF TOTAL 74 METAL OBJECT (IRON)

SL.NO.:-	TYPE:-	NO:-	PESENTAGE:-	PERIOD /DATE:-	IDENTIFICATION
60	IRON SPEARHEAD	: 1	= 1.35 %	III—C 900 B.C.—600 B.C.	HUNTING
61	IRON DAGGER	: 1	= 1.35 %	III—C900 B.C.—600 B.C.	HUNTING/CUTTING

OBSERVATION :- 10.81% OF TOTAL 74 METAL OBJECT (IRON)

SL.NO.:-	TYPE:-	NO:-	PESENTAGE:-	PERIOD /DATE:-	IDENTIFICATION
62-63	SPEARHEAD	:2	= 2.70%	IV —C 600 B.C. —300 B.C.	HUNTING
64-67	DAGGER	:4	= 5.41%	IV —C 600 B.C. —300 B.C.	HUNTING /CUTTING
68	NAIL	:1	= 1.35%	IV —C 600 B.C. —300 B.C.	FOR FIXING
69	DISC	:1	= 1.35%	IV —C 600 B.C. —300 B.C.	PORTION OF CONTAINER

OBSERVATION :- 6.75% OF TOTAL 74 METAL OBJECT (IRON)

SL.NO.:-	TYPE:-	NO:-	PESENTAGE:-	PERIOD /DATE:-	IDENTIFICATION
70	HOOK	:1	= 1.35%	V —C 300 B.C. —200AD.	FOR HUNTING
71	ARROW HEAD	:1	=1.35 %	V—C 300 B.C. —200 AD.	FOR HUNTING
72	ENGRAVER	:1	= 1.35 %	V—C 300 B.C.—200 AD.	FOR INCISION
73	PLATE	:1	=1.35 %	V—C 300 B.C.—200 AD.	PORTION OF CONTAINER
74	SPEAR HEAD	:1	=1.35 %	V—C 300 B.C.—200 AD.	FOR HUNTING

Plate 76

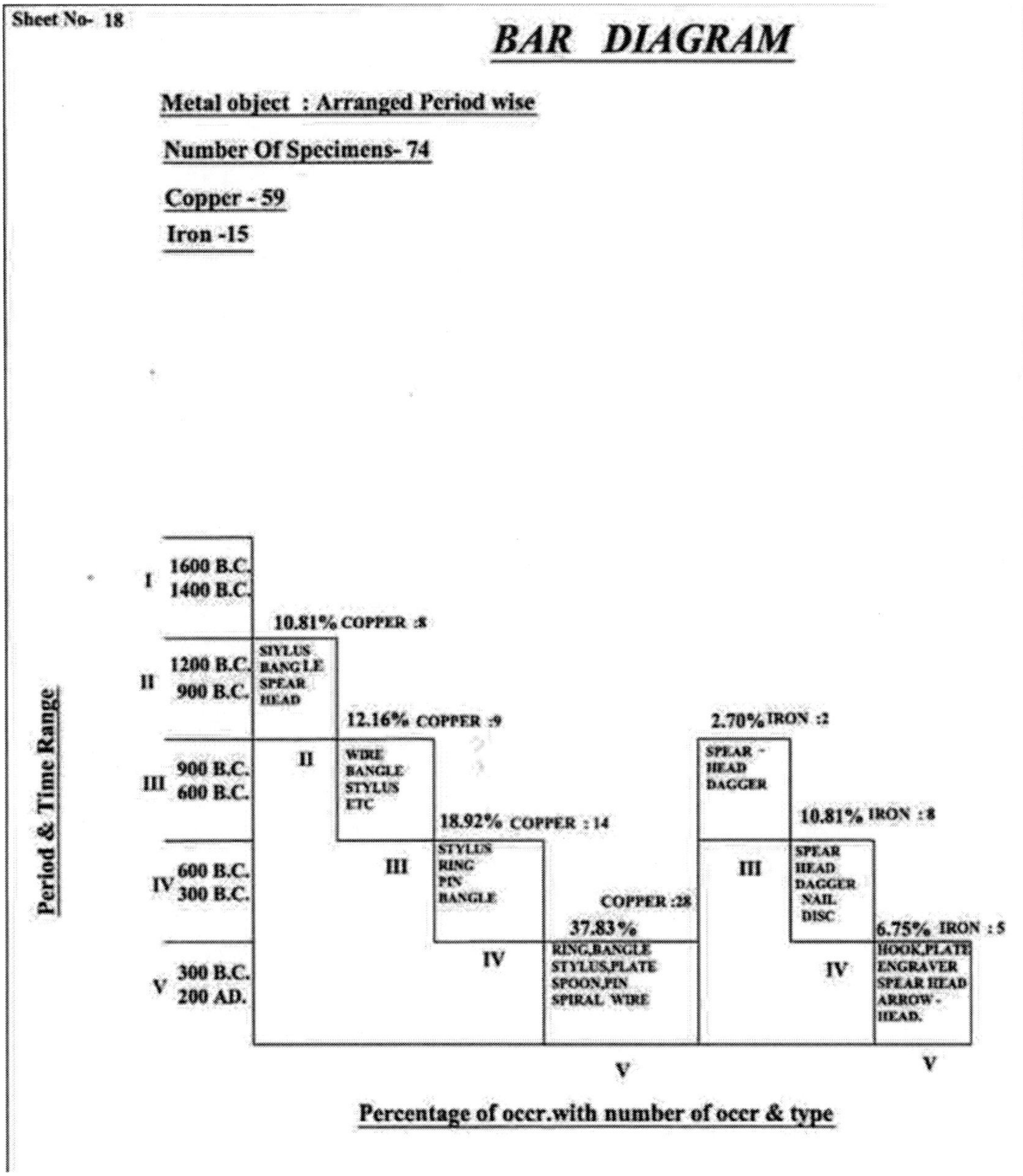
Sheet No- 18
BAR DIAGRAM
Metal object : Arranged Period wise
Number Of Specimens- 74
Copper - 59
Iron -15
Period & Time Range
I 1600 B.C. 1400 B.C.
II 1200 B.C. 900 B.C.
III 900 B.C. 600 B.C.
IV 600 B.C. 300 B.C.
V 300 B.C. 200 AD.
10.81% COPPER :8
SIYLUS BANGLE SPEAR HEAD
II
12.16% COPPER :9
WIRE BANGLE STYLUS ETC
III
18.92% COPPER : 14
STYLUS RING PIN BANGLE
IV
COPPER :28
37.83%
RING,BANGLE STYLUS,PLATE SPOON,PIN SPIRAL WIRE
V
2.70% IRON :2
SPEAR - HEAD DAGGER
III
10.81% IRON : 8
SPEAR HEAD DAGGER NAIL DISC
IV
6.75% IRON : 5
HOOK,PLATE ENGRAVER SPEAR HEAD ARROW - HEAD.
V
Percentage of occr.with number of occr & type

Plate 77

Sheet No- 19

PIE CHART

METAL OBJECT : ARRANGE PERIOD WISE

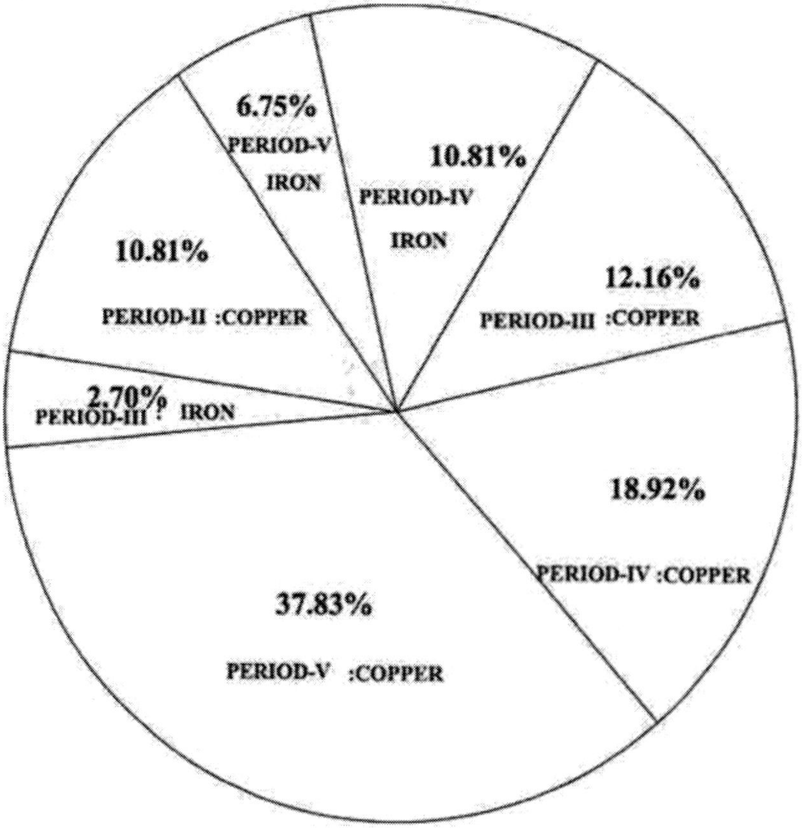

Plate 78

Sheet No- 20

Terracotta Objects Arranged Period Wise

Number Of Specimens- 27, Material:- Terracotta

SL.NO.:-	TYPE:-	NO.OF OCCR&%:-	PERIOD /DATE:-	MATERIAL
1	MALE TORSO	:1 = 3.70%	II —C 1200 B.C. —900 B.C.	HUMAN BEING
2	BEAD	:1 = 3.70%	II —C 1200 B.C. —900 B.C.	ORNAMENT
3	HUMPED BULL	:1 = 3.70 %	III —C 900 B.C. —600 B.C.	ANIMAL
4	BEAD	:1 = 3.70%	III —C 900 B.C. —600 B.C.	ORNAMENT
5	HUMPED BULL	:1 = 3.70 %	IV —C 600 B.C. —300 B.C.	ANIMAL
6	LID	:1 = 3.70%	IV —C 600 B.C. —300 B.C.	HOUSE HOLD ARTICAL
7	MINIATURE DOUBLE EDGE AXE	:1 = 3.70%	IV —C 600 B.C. —300 B.C.	VOTIVE
8-9	DOG	: 2 = 7.41 %	V—C 300 B.C.—200 AD.	ANIMAL
10-13	TORSO	:4 = 14.81%	V —C 300 B.C. —200 AD.	HUMAN BEING
14-18	MOTHER GODDESS	:5 =18.52 %	V—C 300 B.C.—200 AD.	RELATED WITH FERTILITY CULT
19	WAIST UP TO KNEE	: 1 = 3.70 %	V—C 300 B.C. —200 AD.	HUMAN BEING
20	LID	:1 = 3.70%	V —C 300 B.C. —200 AD.	HOUSE HOLD ARTICAL
21	PENDANT	:1 = 3.70%	V —C 300 B.C. —200 AD.	ORNAMENT
22	FIGURINE (WITH STAMP MOTIFS)	:1 = 3.70%	V C 300 B.C. —200 AD.	HUMAN BEING
23	MALE FIGURE	: 1 = 3.70%	V —C 300 B.C.—200 AD.	HUMAN BEING ARTICAL
24	FLESH RUBBER	:1 = 3.70%	V —C 300 B.C. —200 AD.	HOUSE HOLD ARTICAL
25	SEALING (DEPICTING YUPA KASTHA)	: 1 = 3.70%	V—C 300 B.C.—200 AD.	VOTIVE
26	TORTOISE(HEAD)	:1 = 3.70%	V —C 300 B.C. —200 AD.	ANIMAL
27	SLING BOLL	:1 = 3.70%	V—C 300 B.C.—200 AD.	WEAPON

MAJOR TYPE	PERCENTAGE
HUMAN BEING	-8 = 29.63 %
MOTHER GODDESS	-5 = 18.52 %
ORNAMENTS	- 3 = 11.10%
HOUSE HOLD ARTICLE	- 3 = 11.10%
VOTIVE	- 2 = 7.41 %
ANIMEL	- 5 = 18.52 %
WEAPON	- 1 = 3.70%

Plate 79

Sheet No-21

Terracotta Objects Arranged Period Wise

Number Of Specimens- 27, Material:- Terracotta

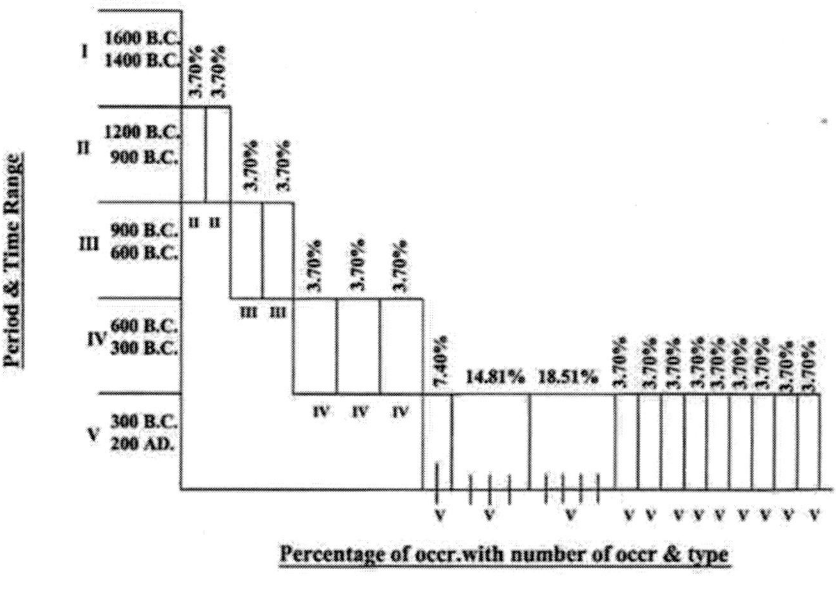

Plate 80

Sheet No- 22

PIE CHART

TERRACOTTA OBJECTS : ARRANGE PERIOD WISE

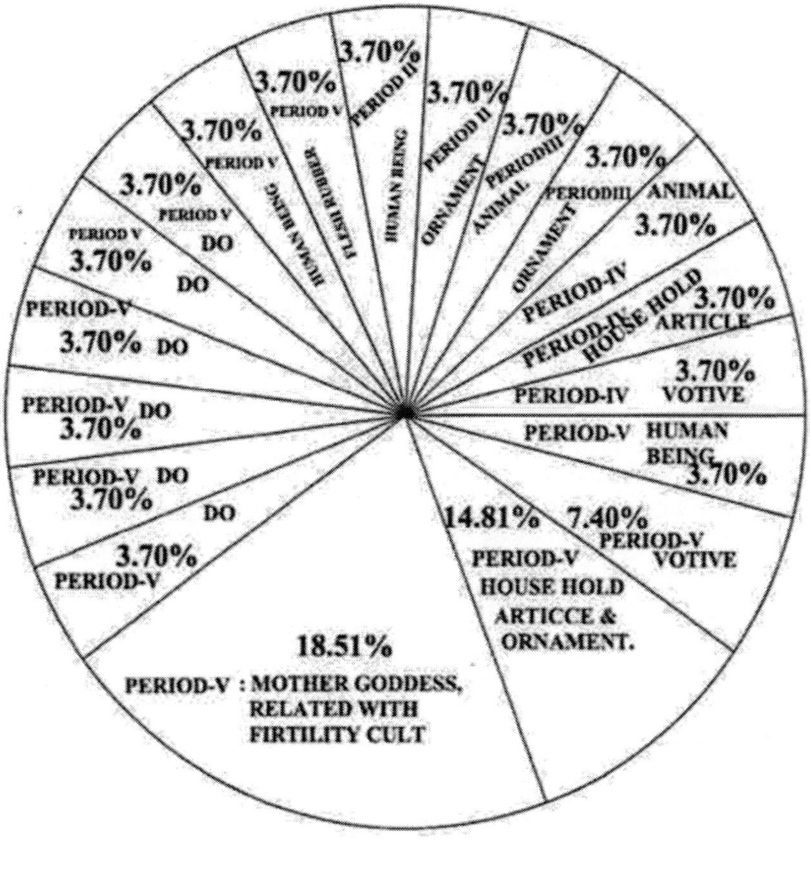

Plate 81

Sheet No- 23

Beads Arranged period wise

Number Of Specimens- 31, Material:- Semi precious stone,Terracotta & copper

SL.NO.:-	TYPE:-	NO:-	PERIOD /DATE:-	MATERIAL
1	TUBULAR	:1	———II —C 1200 B.C. —900 B.C.	COPPER
2	LONG BARREL CIRCULAR	:1	———III —C 900 B.C. —600 B.C.	BANDED QUARTZ
3	SHORT BARREL CIRCULAR	:1	———IV —C 600 B.C. —300 B.C.	AGATE
4	LONG BARREL CIRCULAR	:1	———IV —C 600 B.C. —300 B.C.	AGATE
5	SHORT BARREL CIRCULAR	:1	———IV —C 600 B.C. —300 B.C.	AGATE
6	LONG BARREL CIRCULAR	:1	———IV —C 600 B.C. —300 B.C.	CARNELIAN
7	CORE	:1	———IV —C 600 B.C. —300 B.C.	FELSFSER
8	SPHERICAL	:1	———IV —C 600 B.C. —300 B.C.	CARNEL IAN
9	LONG BARREL CIRCULAR	:1	———IV —C 600 B.C. —300 B.C.	AGATE
10	SHORT BARREL CIRCULAR	:1	———IV —C 600 B.C. —300 B.C.	AGATE
11	SMALL SPHERICAL	:1	———IV —C 600 B.C. —300 B.C.	MILKY QUARTZ
12	SHORT BARREL CIRCULAR	:1	———IV —C 600 B.C. —300 B.C.	BANDED AGATE
13	LONG BARREL CIRCULAR	:1	———V —C 300 B.C. —200 AD.	BANDED AGATE
14	TRIANGULAR	:1	———V —C 300 B.C. —200 AD.	BANDED AGATE
15	SHORT BARREL CIRCULAR	:1	———V —C 300 B.C. —200 AD.	BANDED AGATE
16	SPHERICAL	:1	———V —C 300 B.C. —200 B.C.	BANDED CARNELIAN
17	CONVEX BARREL	:1	———V —C 300 B.C. —200 AD.	BANDED CARNELIAN
18	LONG BARREL CIRCULAR	:1	———V —C 300 B.C. —200 AD.	BANDED CARNELIAN
19	LONG BARREL CIRCULAR	:1	———V —C 300 B.C. —200 AD.	BANDED AGATE
20	LONG BARREL CIRCULAR	:1	———V —C 300 B.C. —200 AD.	BANDED AGATE
21	LONG BARREL CIRCULAR	:1	———V —C 300 B.C. —200 AD.	TERRRACOTTA
22	LONG BARREL CIRCULAR	:1	———V —C 300 B.C. —200 AD.	BANDED CARNELIAN
23	SPHERICAL	:1	———V —C 300 B.C. —200 B.C.	TERRACOTA
24	SPHERICAL	:1	———V —C 300 B.C. —200 B.C.	LAPIS LAZULI
25	SPHERICAL	:1	———V —C 300 B.C. —200 B.C.	CHALCEDONY
26	SPHERICAL	:1	———V —C 300 B.C. —200 B.C.	GREEN STONE
27	SHORT BARREL CIRCULAR	:1	———V —C 300 B.C. —200 AD.	AGATE
28	BUTTON SHAPE, LENTICULAR	:1	———V —C 300 B.C. —200 AD.	AGATE
29	BUTTON SHAPE, LENTICULAR	:1	———V —C 300 B.C. —200 AD.	AGATE
30	TRIANGULAR	:1	———V —C 300 B.C. —200 AD.	BANDED AGATE
31	LOZENGE SHAPE CIRCULAR	:1	———V —C 300 B.C. —200 AD.	STEATITE

Plate 82

Sheet No- 24

Beads Arranged period wise

Number Of Specimens- 31, Material:- Semi precious stone,Terracotta & copper

%Of Period Wise Occurrence Of Beads With The Identification of Core Materials

PERIOD- I = NIL

PERIOD-II = 1 = 3.33% COPPER

PERIOD -III = 1 = BANDED QUARLZ 3.33%

PERIOD-IV =10=BANDED AGATE,QUARTZ,FELSPER,CARNELIAN 32.25%

PERIOD - V = 19 = BANDED AGATE, LAPIS LAZULI, BANDED CARNELIAN, CHALCEDONY, STEATITE, TERRA-COTTA 61.29%

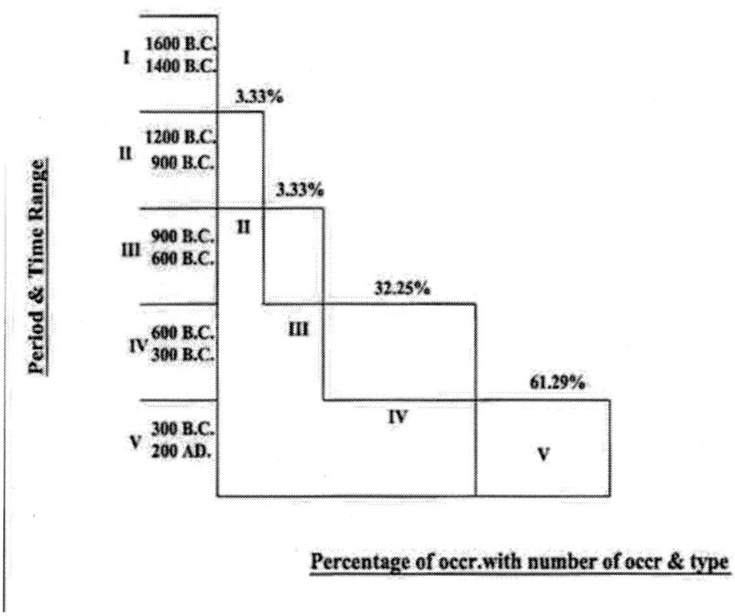

Plate 83

Sheet No- 25

PIE CHART

BEADS : ARRANGE PERIOD WISE

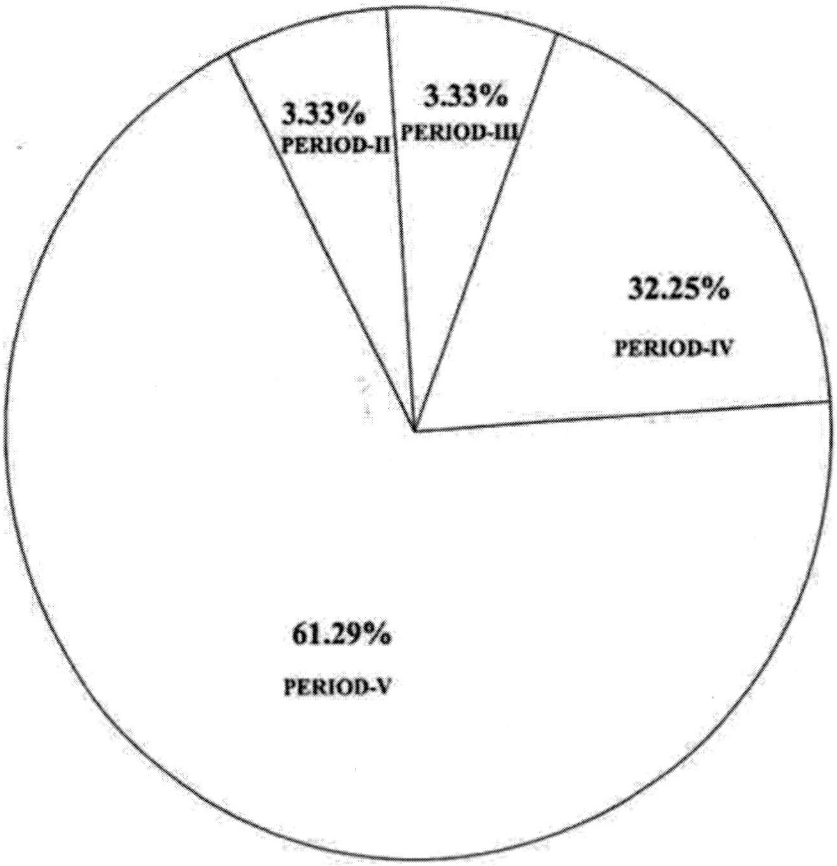

Plate 84

Sheet No- 26

Lithic Implements: Arranged Period Wise

Number Of Specimens- 17

SL.NO.:-	TYPE:-	NO.OF OCCR&%:-	PERIOD /DATE:-	IDENTIFICATION
1-2	MICROLITH	:2 = 11.76%	III —C 900 B.C. —600 B.C.	SCRAPER
3	MICROLITH	:1 = 5.88%	III —C 900 B.C. —600 B.C.	FLUTTED CORE
4	MITROLITH	:1 =5.88 %	IV —C 600 B.C.—300 B.C.	SCRAPER
5-6	MITROLITH	:2 = 11.76%	IV —C 600 B.C.—300 B.C.	POINT
7	MITROLITH	:1 =5.88 %	IV—C 600 B.C.—300 B.C.	BLADE
8	MITROLITH	:1 =5.88 %	IV —C 600 B.C.—300 B.C.	CORE
9	MICROLITH	:1 = 5.88%	V —C 300 B.C. —200 AD.	POINT
10	MICROLITH	:1 = 5.88%	V —C 300 B.C. —200 AD.	BLADE
11-14	POLISHED IMPLEMENTS	:4 = 23.52%	IV C 600 B.C. —300 B.C.	CELT
15-17	POLISHED IMPLEMENTS	:3 = 17.64%	V C 300 B.C. —200 AD.	CELT & PESTLER

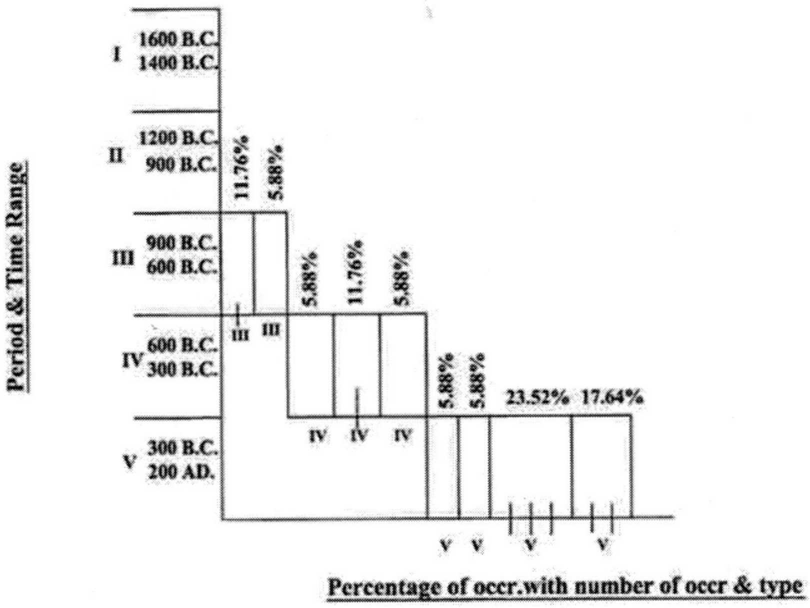

Plate 85

Sheet No- 27

PIE CHART

LITHIC OBJECTS :ARRANGE PERIOD WISE

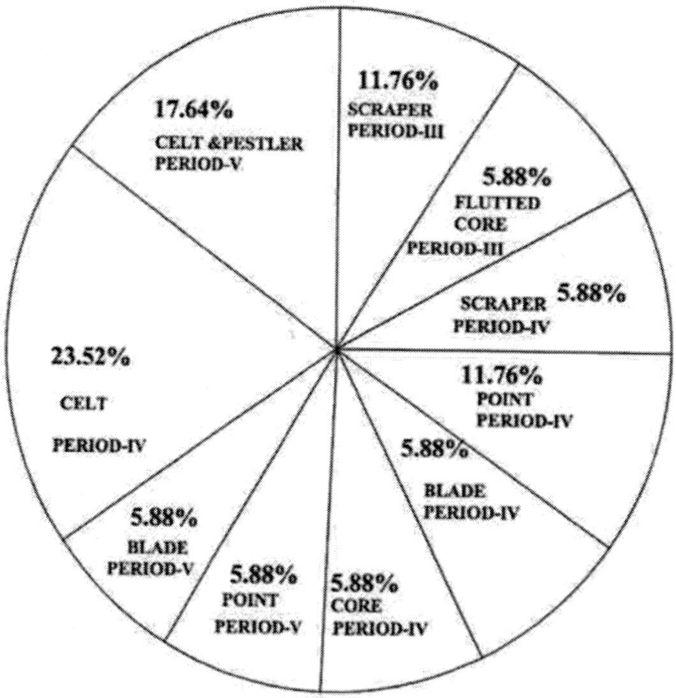